Winston S. Churchill

Edward

Haïle Selassé I R.R.

[Amharic script]

[Amharic script] E. yhaye

1915.

30-VI-31

George Wyndham.

Constantine R.

September 1913

Nellie Melba

22. 7. 13.

Maximilian, Prinz von Hessen.

Elizabeth Cooper

22nd February 2012

GRAND HOTEL

Peter Pugh

GRAND HOTEL EASTBOURNE

This edition published in 2000 by Cambridge Business Publishing
Grange Road, Duxford, Cambridge CB2 4QF
Previously published in 1987 by The Grand Hotel, Eastbourne
Copyright © 1987, 2000 Peter Pugh

ISBN: 1 84046 228 0

Printed and bound in the UK by Butler and Tanner Ltd., Frome.

ACKNOWLEDGEMENTS

It was a great thrill to be asked to research and write the history of such a wonderful hotel as the Grand, and of course I have not suffered too many privations while staying in the hotel to carry out the research.

In writing a history it is important to have the constant help and support of the management, and at the Grand these have been forthcoming at every turn. Peter Hawley and Jonathan Webley both took a great personal interest in the project and were available at any time to give me assistance.

It is invidious to give a list of names, as so many have been helpful, but I would like to mention the following:

Mrs David Sachs who lent the autograph book of her father, Mr Van Lier,

Mrs Michelle Jenkins, wife of the late Tom Jenkins, and Mrs Jill Byfield, wife of the late Jack Byfield, both of whom were so helpful over the musical history of the Grand,

Mrs Violet Watt, daughter of the former managers, Mr and Mrs Sam Eeley, who lent her parents' visitors book,

Mr and Mrs Tom Jones who again helped with the musical background,

Mrs Alice Riding who lent three comprehensive scrap books,

Miss Marie Lewis at the Eastbourne Library who was the fount of all knowledge on Eastbourne and who also provided many photographs,

All the present staff and many of the former staff of the hotel who were extremely kind and helpful in providing information to build a picture of the hotel.

The extract on page 73 from Britain In Our Century *by Arthur Marwick (© 1984 Arthur Marwick) is reproduced by permission of Thames and Hudson.*

The extract from Slightly Foxed *by Angela Fox (© 1986 Angela Fox) on page 191 concerning Mrs Grade is reproduced by permission of William Collins, Sons & Co. Ltd.*

CONTENTS

FOREWORD

by the Duke of Devonshire P.C. M.C.

My family has always been very proud of its long connection with Eastbourne, indeed the 7th Duke must take much of the credit for creating the town as it is today. If I was asked to describe Eastbourne's outstanding quality I would choose the word excellence and if this can be used about the borough as a whole it can certainly be used to describe the Grand Hotel. Whatever the season, to enter its portals lifts the spirits. It is particularly gratifying to me to find the first room on the left named after my Derbyshire home. The fame of the Grand was in past decades spread far and wide since the BBC music programme "Grand Hotel" first came from the Grand's orchestra.

Since my family ceased to live at Compton Place, whenever I go to Eastbourne, which is as often as possible, I spend the night at the Grand. The pace is calm and leisured and, lulled by the luxury and comfort, I find my problems disappearing and the world a better place to live in. No wonder it is necessary to book weeks ahead to be sure of getting a room. The Grand is surely the jewel in Eastbourne's splendid crown.

INTRODUCTION

This is the story of one of the great hotels in the British Isles.

It was built in 1875 when Great Britain was still expanding its Empire and when no one questioned who ruled the land – the upper classes did. Those upper classes by and large took their holidays by the sea in this country and for many weeks, even months, at a time. They employed servants and nannies for their children and took some of them on holiday with them. The Grand was built to cater for all of them.

The story covers a century of great change. The First World War, the Kaiser's War as some called it, changed society drastically. The Grand itself had a prosperous war and enjoyed an Indian summer into the 1920s with very little changed from its former style. The 1930s brought harder times and the Second World War, Hitler's War, was entirely different from the Kaiser's War.

Eastbourne, easy prey for the Germans across the Channel, suffered continuous air raids, and the Grand along with all others was closed down as a hotel. Nevertheless, it contributed to the war effort by housing different sections of the invading forces.

After the war, thanks to heroic efforts by Dick Beattie and his staff, the Grand picked itself up again and gradually re-established itself as one of the finest hotels in the country. The old style of guest had virtually disappeared, but the hotel adapted itself to the modern needs of business visitors for most of the year and private guests for holiday periods.

Over the Grand's first 125 years, many famous guests have experienced its outstanding hospitality – musicians, royalty, singers, actors, sports stars and tycoons. I hope you will enjoy reading about them and their foibles and will feel some of the relaxed atmosphere which the Grand has always endeavoured to provide.

CHAPTER ONE

WHO BUILT THE HOTEL, AND WHY?

WHO BUILT THE HOTEL AND WHY? ————————

There is some controversy over the building of the Grand Hotel. Mr Leonard Earp, who still lives near Eastbourne, was brought up by his grandmother Jane Earp in the belief that his grandfather William Earp built the Grand Hotel as a private residence for themselves and their 13 children. According to Jane Earp they subsequently moved to Cliffe House which they built on the hillside above the Grand towards Beachy Head. When this new house was completed, William Earp wanted to sell his original house, the Grand, and as he felt the only use for it was as a hotel he wanted permission to turn it into one. The Duke of Devonshire, the original owner of the land, refused this permission whereupon William Earp resorted to the courts. Earp won his case and the Grand was able to be sold with permission to use it as a hotel.

This story does not quite ring true. William Earp undoubtedly sued the Duke of Devonshire in court but this was probably over the building of a road to his house, the Cliffe.

The foundations of the Grand being laid. At this stage the hotel was on the edge of the development of Eastbourne.

The Grand was almost certainly always intended as a hotel and was built that way. The *Eastbourne Gazette's* report on Wednesday, 13 May 1874 lends credence to this view,

> If also, we are informed aright, a gentleman already owning a large mansion in Eastbourne, has matured a scheme which will dwarf all previous attempts at hotel accommodation in the town. Several thousand pounds have already been expended in the purchase of the site, which is at the extreme west of the Grand Parade, between Mostyn Terrace and Cliff House, near the Burlington Park. Upon this site is proposed to erect a magnificent hotel at a cost of £40,000 or £50,000 the frontage being 400 ft. The hotel will contain 200 bedrooms and every elaboration and convenience of a first-class establishment, while two acres of ground in the rear will be laid out for the use of visitors, and as conservatories. The preparation of the plans have been entrusted to our townsman, Mr R.K. Blessley, and

The view looking towards Beachy Head in 1870. William Earp's Cliffe House ("Earp's Folly") has already been built.

The view towards Beachy Head after the Grand and other houses had been built.

there is no doubt that if the project is carried out the hotel will bear a most favourable comparison with any similar establishment on the south coast...

Furthermore, the Sussex directories of the time suggest that William Earp lived at the Cliffe and managed the Grand Hotel. The 1874 directory mentions the following hotels — Cavendish, Albion, Gildridge, Diplock, Burlington, Sussex and Anchor, but not the Grand. In fact, whereas Mr W. Earp is mentioned as living in the Cliffe in the 1877 Gowlands Eastbourne postal directory it is not until 1878 that we get the following insertion,

The Grand Hotel, at the south-west end of Cliff Road, is a classical erection, overlooking the sea, stands on three acres and was completed in 1877, and has a large dining hall and drawing room, besides a large hall 40 feet square and 46 feet in height.

It also has an entry — "William Earp — Grand Hotel"

An early view of the Grand without either the East or West Wing.

The original planning application for the Grand, which shows quite clearly that William Earp always intended the Grand to be a hotel.

A study of the plans submitted by William Earp to the local authorities confirms that the Grand was always intended as a hotel.

What is not in doubt is that the architect was Robert Knott Blessley who also designed Lushington Road and Leaf Hall in Eastbourne. Nor is there any doubt that the hotel at this stage consisted only of the central part without either of the wings.

THE HOTEL COMES INTO BEING

What is also not in doubt is that the Grand Hotel was designed from the outset to be in the luxury class. An advertisement in

Robert Knott Blessley — the hotel architect.

Leaf Hall — another of Blessley's designs. The contrast with the Grand is quite marked.

the 1886 Gowland Directory describes its amenities

— this magnificent hotel facing the sea stands in its own Ornamental Grounds with Tennis lawn at the west end or most fashionable part of Eastbourne in close proximity to the Devonshire Park and Baths and within a few minutes' drive of the railway station.

— it contains over 200 rooms including a Grand Dining Saloon and Drawing Room, Library, Conservatory, Sitting Rooms with private balconies overlooking the sea and bedrooms en suite, Billiard and Smoke rooms, lavatories, etc. [It is difficult to imagine a luxury hotel in 1986 advertising the fact that it had lavatories!]

— it has a Hydraulic Lift to every floor and is replete with every modern appliance for the comfort of visitors.

—special attention has recently been given to the Sanitary arrangements which are now quite perfect and a new handsomely fitted Lavatory has been added on the ground floor. [The hotel obviously had some problems with lavatories in its early years.]

By 1890 the directory was prepared to praise the hotel fulsomely,

There are several very fine hotels at Eastbourne, notably the Grand Hotel near the Wish Tower. It stands in its own grounds directly facing the sea and within a stone's throw of the Devonshire Park and Baths and offers every requisite for luxury, convenience and comfort. The building contains over 200 rooms; increased accommodation for nearly a 100 visitors, new Turkish Baths, smoking, billiard rooms having recently been added. The carriage drive on the sea front is being done away with and a handsome lawn front is being carefully laid out. The arrival and departure entrance is now in the Compton Street front where a fine row of shops has been erected on the building. A post and telegraph office has also just been opened in the hotel — a great convenience to the neighbourhood as well as to visitors. Sanitary arrangements are perfect. There is an Hydraulic Lift to each floor and in the winter months the hotel is warmed throughout by hot water pipes.

Bath chair man outside the hotel in the 1880s. The bath chair men flourished up until the Second World War, taking guests up and down the promenade.

7

Mr Richard Crook, an architect in Eastbourne in the 1980s, is also fulsome in his praise of both the Eastbourne of the nineteenth century and of the Grand Hotel,

> The Grand has that exclusive air typical of Victorian Eastbourne and its brilliant stucco facades are enriched with precise cornices, brackets and urns, giving the appearance of an icing sugar palace when viewed under a starry sky on a warm summer evening . . . Eastbourne is a unique example of a planned and zoned Victorian aristocratic seaside development. It is beautifully laid out, with its wide tree-lined streets, elegant squares, terraces, hotels and villas. It must surely deserve its 19th century title 'The Empress of Watering Places'.

Eastbourne itself has an interesting history, which can be summarised to put the Grand in its context.

THE EARLY DAYS OF EASTBOURNE

In the Domesday Book in 1086 Eastbourne appears as Bourne with Robert, the Earl of Mortain holding the land for the King.

Domesday Sussex — Eastbourne appeared as Bourne and was not as significant as Pevensey.

Robert was in fact William the Conqueror's half-brother. The Normans divided the country into Rapes each with a river for trading and a castle for defence. Eastbourne was in the Rape of Pevensey as Pevensey was a more significant settlement in those days. The Earl of Mortain's estate was passed down through the centuries until in the eighteenth century a Lady Elizabeth Compton, who had inherited part of it, married Lord George Cavendish, the third son of the Duke of Devonshire. This brought the Compton Estate into the Cavendish family.

Jesus House, Church Street, — perhaps the oldest building in Eastbourne.

The recently restored Lambe Inn, which was built in the seventeenth century.

SMUGGLING AND FISHING ──────────

The Devonshire family played a major role in the development of Eastbourne in the nineteenth century and indeed in the building of the Grand Hotel in the 1870s, but before this age when Eastbourne became "a town built by a gentleman for gentlemen" the area was a little less tranquil.

In the early nineteenth century the whole population in the area around Eastbourne seemed to be involved in smuggling. Dragoons were brought in to hunt them down but in the event they made friends with the locals and proved to be of little use to the Excise officers. The fishermen also seemed happy to involve themselves with the smugglers and adopted nicknames or codenames — "Killcraft", "Alligator" and "Cateyes". These were used to confuse the Excise men and indeed the tradition continued long after smuggling died away. For all its romantic overtones smuggling became a serious business for both sides and on one occasion a customs officer was found shot dead with seven bullets in his body.

The Redoubt, which was built along with the Wish Tower as part of the Martello Towers defence scheme against the threat of invasion by Napoleon. The army and their families brought some prosperity to the town to be followed by a slump when they departed after Waterloo in 1815.

The profitable goods to smuggle were brandy, tobacco, tea and fine silk. Ingenious methods were devised. For example ladies' elbow length silk gloves were screwed up and put into an empty walnut shell with the two sides of the shell then being stuck together. Kegs of brandy were hidden in various places such as the windmill at Polegate. Another favourite hiding place was the stream which ran into the sea just west of the

Wish Tower. One of the penalties if captured was for the offending boat to be brought ashore and cut in half by the revenue officers.

As the nineteenth century progressed smuggling declined and legitimate fishing became a more significant occupation.

THE DEVELOPMENT OF EASTBOURNE ————

Eastbourne was already recognised by some as a pleasant place to take a holiday — King George III sent his son, Prince Edward and several of his daughters here for four months in 1780 "for the sea bathing and other advantages the place has to offer." William Wilberforce, who was to battle long and hard against the slave trade, came here with his family in 1808, as did Lord

Compton Place — the home of the Dukes of Devonshire in the nineteenth century.

Opposite: *William Cavendish, seventh Duke of Devonshire — the man who did so much to develop Eastbourne in the 1860s, 70s and 80s.*

Tennyson in 1845. Nevertheless, the population in 1851 was still only 3,000. It was in the 1850s that the real development occurred. As with all such rapid developments growth was not smooth. Boom conditions in the 1850s were followed by a slump in the 1860s and a further boom in the 1870s. The population had grown to 10,361 by 1871 and to 34,278 by 1891. Eastbourne became the fastest growing town in Sussex.

The Duke of Devonshire was a significant figure in this development and was sufficiently involved to note in his diary in April 1873,

A good many buildings are going on or will shortly begin.

And again in 1876,

There seems every prospect of the place continuing to prosper.

The *Eastbourne Gazette* waxed rather more lyrical in 1875,

Brilliant as has been the last ten years of Eastbourne's existence, its sun of success has only just dawned, and will rise higher and higher as years move on, bathing its enterprising inhabitants in floods of golden light ... Cornfields and barns have given place to substantial shops and dwelling houses, almost from one end of the parish to the other.

Kitty Quill — the flower seller. Note her "By appointment" badge. She did not let anyone forget she had sold flowers to the Princess of Wales.

Bathing machines — men and women used separate parts of the beach. These machines were up-ended, filled with sand and used as barricades against invasion in 1940.

The birdcage bandstand, with the paddle steamer in the background.

GRAND PARADE EASTBOURNE.

In the 1880s to the west of the Wish Tower the Duke of Devonshire financed the extension of parades towards Holywell and also the building of scenic roads to Beachy Head. The *Gazette* was not slow to respond,

> The West of the town is increasing with marvellous rapidity, and the magnificent series of terraces reaching to Holywell furnishes a choice of promenades unrivalled for beauty and extent in England.

The 1870s saw the building of the Queen's Hotel, Cavendish Hotel and Grand Hotel and of the Devonshire Club for the town's most important residents and visitors. In 1873 the Devonshire Parks and Baths Company was formed and in 1874 the baths and floral hall were opened.

The Devonshire Baths, designed by the brilliant civil engineer, G.A. Wallis, were the largest heated, salt-water baths

The Prince and Princess of Wales taking tea at Compton Place after they had opened Western Parade and the Princess Alice Hospital in June 1883.

in the country. Wallis used the natural tidal rise and fall to fill and empty the baths via a cast-iron pipe under Grand Parade.

In 1876 the first concert was held in the Pavilion and in 1884 the theatre was built. After the pier was partly destroyed in a storm in 1877, it was rebuilt on a more lavish scale the following year. Flower shows and regattas took place and in 1882 electric lighting was erected on the sea-front.

On 30 June 1883 the Prince and Princess of Wales visited the town to open Western Parade and the Princess Alice Hospital. Princess Alice, Queen Victoria's third child, born in 1843, had married Prince Louis of Hesse and had become greatly interested in caring for the sick after the misery she saw in the Austro-Prussian War of 1866. She entered into correspondence with Florence Nightingale and during the last year of her life which she spent in Eastbourne she spent as much time as she could in visiting the old and infirm. She died in 1878 of diphtheria at the young age of 35 and the people of Eastbourne remembered her by naming their new hospital after her. (Incidentally, her daughter Alexandra was the Tsarina of Russia executed with the Tsar and the rest of their family in 1917.)

This hectic activity was followed by another slump at the end of the 1880s epitomised by the bankruptcy of one of the town's foremost builders, Ruben Climpson. But in the 1890s growth was resumed and the population increased further to 51,554 by 1907. In terms of population therefore Eastbourne had grown 17 times in just over fifty years. Train services were improved so that it became easier for visitors from not only London but also the Midlands and North. The facilities of Devonshire Park were extended and a full-time orchestra was established. (Brighton and Bournemouth had long had one.) The Eighth Duke of Devonshire served as mayor in 1897 and the Ninth Duke in 1909 (his inaugural dinner was held at the Grand Hotel and was a magnificent affair). "The Empress of Watering Places has secured one of the foremost subjects as its First Citizen."

55 EASTBOURNE. — Railway Station. — LL.

Eastbourne Railway Station 1886 — the improved services to London, the Midlands and the North were important for the Grand Hotel.

Both Edward VII and George V came to Eastbourne as friends of the Dukes of Devonshire.

By 1911, Brighton was still on its own as the country's leading resort with a population of 150,000 but Eastbourne was firmly established alongside Scarborough, Bournemouth, Blackpool and Southport. Others such as Hastings, Torquay and Folkestone had been left well behind. The service provided is typified by the fact that in the 1890s vans would carry sea-water — hot or cold — to any part of the town. Hot water cost 3d a bucket and cold 2d a bucket. It also happened to have the first municipal omnibus service which ran from the Meads to the railway station.

This was the backdrop for the hotel. How was it faring in its early days?

Eastbourne's earliest motor bus with members of the Town Council including Alderman Maude, who did so much to establish the corporation's bus services.

THE GRAND IN ITS EARLY DAYS————————

In the 1881 directory an advertisement listed these features:

Turkish Bath
Private Omnibus meets all the trains
Short-hand and type-writers office
Library and public rooms lighted with electric light
No charge for attendance
Table d'hôte (separate tables) 6.30-8.00 pm
New Golf Links within ten minutes walk

Several interesting points emerge from these entries. The hydraulic lift was clearly a sufficiently novel feature to make it worthy of mention. The presence of carriages was probably

The Compton Street entrance to the hotel with the shops being added in 1887.

The Compton Street entrance to the hotel in the 1970s.

considered a nuisance on the stretch of ground between the hotel and the sea and the management decided to change the entrance to Compton Street (as we shall see the entrance stayed in Compton Street at what is now the back of the hotel until the 1950s). Central heating would also have been an unusual feature for a hotel in the late nineteenth century and clearly so was electric light to warrant a specific mention in an advertisement.

Perhaps the most interesting remark in the advertisement is the "table d'hôte (separate tables)". Most hotels offered one or several large tables where the guests all mixed together, very often with the proprietor or manager sitting down to dinner with his or her guests. The mention of the new golf links reminds us that this was the period when golf was just becoming a craze with Victorian gentry and courses were springing up all over the British Isles.

The central heating was only added in the 1880s because when the hotel opened in 1878 there had been no telephones, no central heating and indeed no hot and cold running water. There were only six bathrooms to cater for 200 rooms. The chambermaids would put brass cans of hot water in each room before lunch and dinner.

A report by two electrical engineers from London, Messrs Mordey and Dawbarn in 1902, shows that electric lighting was gradually installed in the hotel from 1886 onwards. In that year it was first installed in the entrance and the lounge.

EARLY MANAGERS

Apart from the confusion over William Earp and the building of the Grand Hotel there seems to have been a certain amount of instability in the early days concerning both the management and ownership of the hotel. In Gowland's Directory the managers are listed,

1882	W. Earp
1884	J.R. Cleave
1886 – 1890	T. Platten
1891 – 1895	F. Wright
1896	Leversage
1897	G.F. Taylor
1898 – 1904	does not give a name
1905 – 1909	W.F.R. Hagemann
1910	S. Eeley

As we shall see, Sam Eeley remained as manager until the late 1930s and there have only been four since 1946. However in these early days there were plenty of changes as indeed there were in the ownership of the hotel.

In 1896 there was a radical change in the ownership of the hotel when the share capital was greatly increased and the company became a public company with several hundred shareholders. The trading accounts and balance sheets show that the hotel was profitable, making around £20,000 in the late 1890s and early 1900s. This was an acceptable return on a turnover of around £65,000 though perhaps not as exciting when the return on capital employed of £250,000 was considered.

The figures overleaf showing details of income highlight a few points of interest. The 1890s was a strong growth period with turnover rising from just under £21,000 in 1888 to £65,000 in 1900. However the growth then stopped abruptly, probably partly as a result of the Boer War, and turnover was lower in the twelve months to September 1903 than it had been in 1900.

It is interesting to see that fires were charged for as indeed were ordinary baths, as well, of course, as Turkish Baths. Cigars in 1900 were consumed at a percentage of 2.6% to room lettings. If the same held true today the guests would have to buy £37,600 of cigars each year; in fact they buy less then £3,000 (The Boer War seemed to have caused a sharp fall in the cigar consumption — it fell by nearly a third from 1900 to 1903. Perhaps some guests felt it was ostentatious to smoke them while a war was being fought.

As a percentage of room costs the sale of wines and spirits at over 33% was also amazingly high particularly as the tax on alcohol was much lower in the 1890s than it is now. By today's standards the total figures are almost unbelievably low. The annual income from letting bedrooms of less than £20,000 would be passed in two days in 2000.

THE TAP

The Tap, which was earning the hotel around £1,000 in the early 1900s, was the bar which was operated as a concession. In 1890 an agreement was drawn up whereby a Thomas Young and Joseph John Rawley were allowed to sell beer, wines and spirits in the bar of the hotel. The two men bought the stock and any new stock required and gave the hotel 10% of their gross takings. Licensing hours were more liberal — some would say more sensible — in those days. The agreement stipulated that,

> The said Thomas Young and Joseph John Rawley shall open for the convenience of the public the said Tap at the hour of Eight o'clock in the morning and shall close the said Tap at Ten o'clock at night.

It is not surprising that the 1890s saw a steady increase in business as the East Wing of the hotel had been added in 1890. At the same time the Prince's Wing on the ground floor had also been added to provide a banqueting suite for 100 people at private functions. This capacity was considered adequate for private parties in Eastbourne at that time.

Grand Hotel — Income 1888–1903

	1888 £	1889 £	1897 £	1898 £	1899 £	1900 £	1901 £	1902 £	1903 £
Apartments	5,953	7,294	10,596	13,128	15,304	19,081	19,391	19,135	18,679
Firing	267	327	475	588	686	825	855	905	753
Lights	164	201	292	362	422	541	518	511	454
Board	9,237	11,319	16,442	20,371	23,748	29,148	30,163	20,041	28,910
″ Servants	636	780	1,133	1,403	1,636	1,992	1,808	1,893	1,557
Wines & Spirits	2,258	2,767	4,019	4,979	5,805	6,859	6,842	6,467	6,294
Mineral Waters	452	553	804	996	1,160	1,450	1,448	1,406	1,331
Malt Liquors	174	214	311	385	449	556	558	457	490
Cigars	156	191	278	344	401	495	413	347	338
Bicycles	55	68	99	122	142	174	143	113	81
Baths	226	277	402	498	580	701	770	739	694
″ Turkish	96	118	172	213	248	309	396	329	332
Paid Out	160	196	285	353	412	506	469	365	378
Laundry	203	249	362	448	522	641	620	601	526
Billiards	51	63	91	113	132	163	113	123	100
Omnibus	80	98	143	177	206	257	273	294	289
Carriage Hire	117	143	208	258	301	368	492	469	370
Sundries	29	35	51	63	74	94	68	99	110
Tap	246	277	438	543	633	790	685	1,045	934
Total	20,527	25,154	36,539	45,268	52,773	64,952	66,025	64,284	62,620
Rents	192	625	767	839	793	631	631	631	590
Fire Agency	11	4	17	22	31	28	35	41	45
Grand Total	20,781	25,783	37,323	46,135	53,598	65,612	66,691	64,956	63,255

CHAPTER TWO

THE EARLY 1900s

THE ECONOMIC AND SOCIAL SITUATION IN 1900 ———————————————

Edward VII succeeded to the throne on the death of Queen Victoria in 1901. As we know Edward had endured a long spell as Prince of Wales and Victoria had endured a long spell of Edward's indiscretions as Prince of Wales. Nevertheless Edward was generally popular and was the last monarch to give his name to an era — "the Edwardian era". It was a time of some change in the fabric of society though the classes were well defined. In the late nineteenth century the older landed class had amalgamated with the top professional and business people to form what was known in the Edwardian period as the upper class. This class had a virtual monopoly of political power, it dominated business and finance and possessed two thirds of the country's wealth. Theirs was the world of Eton and Harrow, Oxford and Cambridge, Ascot and Henley, country house parties and debutante balls. It was to be hoped it was the world of the Grand Hotel also.

The coachmen resplendent in their hats and buttoned coats outside their hut in front of the hotel. The King of Spain was so impressed with this cabstand that he had an exact replica built in Madrid.

The patrons of the Grand at this time had servants. Keeping houses clean in those days was not the relatively simple occupation it is today. There were no detergents, no vacuum cleaners and virtually no central heating. It was a case of spit and polish and humping buckets of coal around. The divide between master and mistress and their servants was absolute and well-defined and in the large world of domestic service — at 2,600,000 it was the country's largest source of employment — the hierarchy amongst servants was well defined too. At the Grand Hotel it was assumed that most families would bring their servants and therefore special rooms both for sleeping and for their use during the day were set aside for them. There were also special rates for them.

When we see the sales and profit figures in the ensuing pages and the charges for staying the night at the Grand and can perhaps hardly believe how low they are, we must remember that the average weekly wage of women in industrial work in the "golden" Edwardian era was 11s 7d (less than 60p) and the average male wage was only three times as high. (Equal opportunities for the sexes did not exist in those days and, of course, women did not even have the right to vote.)

As we shall see Ernest Page, the Chairman of the Grand Hotel, referred to "nigger minstrels" in a public meeting in 1913. This appears shocking today but it did not in 1913 when law enforcement was liberally, if that is the right word, sprinkled with hanging, flogging, birching and penal servitude. We must remember that the suffragettes suffered force-feeding and the "cat and mouse" tactics of release when on the point of death through starvation and re-arrest when recovered.

The early years of the Edwardian era were in fact years of a struggling economy and hotels, especially luxury hotels, did not find it easy to fill their rooms throughout the year. The Grand Hotel was no exception and constantly in his annual reports the Chairman, Francis Heseltine, spoke of the poor state of business generally. In his 1902 address he also bewailed that unreliable element, the British summer,

> the receipts from all sources shew a slight falling off from that of the previous year, but when we remember the cold and cruel summer which put a stop to many persons visiting the country . . .

He also blamed an unusual event,

> . . . or the intense anxiety and depression of the nation at the alarming illness of the King, which caused the cancellation of the Coronation until almost the middle of the holiday season, can it be wondered that the business of this or any other hotel was disturbed or lessened?

The King had appendicitis which developed into peritonitis. Such was communication, or lack of it, in 1902 that many parts of the country did not know the Coronation had been postponed and celebrated it anyway. They celebrated it again a few weeks later proving that technological progress does not always bring greater happiness.

Nevertheless, the Grand Hotel made sufficient profit in 1902 for the dividend to shareholders to be raised to 10% from 9% and this was after payment of tax. 1902 was also an important year in that Mr Edward Beckwith retired as Chairman. Beckwith had been Chairman since the early 1880s and a constant element in the difficult, formative years of the hotel. He was replaced on the Board by a local man, Mr Ashley Maude who was a member of Eastbourne's Town Council. The Board obtained the approval of the shareholders to spend 500 guineas (perhaps £10,000 today) on a portrait of himself by an eminent artist. In the event Mr Beckwith would not accept this, indeed did not want "to receive any acknowledgement beyond our respect and esteem" but was persuaded to accept a gift in a different form provided the balance was set aside for the benefit of employees of the hotel. Finally Mr Beckwith was presented with a Loving Cup, suitably inscribed, and a pair of antique candlesticks. £400 was put into the fund for employees.

REDECORATION OF THE HALL AND LOUNGE

Redecoration of the Hall and Lounge was carried out in 1903 as nothing had been done in this area for fifteen years. "A decorative artist of the highest standing", Mr Lewis Foreman Day, was commissioned to carry out the work. Clearly his work did not meet with unanimous approval as the Chairman felt obliged to comment in his annual address,

> This (the new decorations) you have perhaps seen and, I hope, admired. Of course, in all matters of art, each person claims, and is

entitled to, his or her own opinion, or may I venture to say 'fad'? The entire obliteration in the new decoration of all that had become familiar to the eye of those who visit the Hotel, has naturally led to considerable criticism. I leave it then to each of you (and I hope you will go and see it) to form your own conclusions, all I would impress upon you is to give no hasty opinion until you have carefully studied the design and realised the difficulties to be overcome, and when you feel sufficiently educated up to the artist's idea, I believe you will agree with me that the work is well conceived and is in all respects worthy of great admiration.

One person who clearly did not think the work worthy of great admiration was the man who was to succeed Heseltine as Chairman and who was to remain Chairman until the 1930s, Ernest Page. In his address to shareholders in 1913 he was scathing about the 1903 decorations,

I have also referred to the decoration of the hall and lounge, on which a large sum was spent. I think now it is a beautiful place. Instead of being a sort of dirty grey with hives down the columns, which used to be compared to the trousers of nigger minstrels, the whole thing is white and gold. In addition to that, instead of the ugly and some-what ancient electroliers and electric lamps which were on the walls, we have very beautiful sconces, I think they are called, put round the walls with electric lights, and also we have a very fine electrolier hanging from the roof.

This was probably the splendid chandelier which hung in the lounge until it was presented to the Devonshire Park Theatre in 1984.

THE WEST WING

Although the completion of the West Wing, that is the self-contained suites on the first, second and third floors, had been planned for 1900, there had been continual delays. It took until

Opposite: *Early etching of the hotel lounge.*

Above: *The dining room — tails and long evening gowns were mandatory. Indeed, no one would ever have thought of anything else.*

the end of 1902 for the plans, drawn up by the architects Hunt and Steward, to be approved by the Corporation as they had to receive the approval of the Grand's neighbours. By then the Board were viewing the general outlook with some trepidation and plans for completion were deferred again. It was not until the end of 1904 that the Board decided to proceed with these rooms and even then part of the capital was raised by the issue of more shares — 4,000 at a premium of £1 over the £5 price to raise £24,000. By the time of the Annual General Meeting in 1905 the work was in hand and completion was expected by the autumn of 1906. In the event the new suites in the West Wing were finally completed in the early part of 1907.

THE FIRING OF THE MANAGER, MR HAGEMANN

Whether the protracted building of the West Wing contributed to the mental breakdown of the manager, Mr. Hagemann, we shall never know, but the Board were forced to ask him to leave immediately at the beginning of the 1906 season. Fortunately a suitable replacement was quickly found in the form of Sam Eeley, who with his very capable wife acted as manager and housekeeper until the late 1930s.

THE APPOINTMENT OF VAN LIER/VON LEER

We shall see in the chapters on music at the Grand Hotel how important the orchestra became in the life and popularity of the hotel. Suffice it to say here that in 1903 a Mr Von Leer was appointed to lead his string orchestra in the lounge. The Chairman put it like this,

We inform you of the engagement of Herr von Leer's string orchestra. I believe you will agree with us that music (especially that of a high class) is now considered almost an essential requirement for hotels of the character of the "Grand". If so, I am sure you will approve of the engagement of this orchestra which plays daily in the Hall, afternoon and evening. It is admitted by all who have heard it to be one of great merit and considerable note and has, so far, proved an attraction and has given great pleasure to the visitors, as is evidenced by the applause with which their music is greeted. Some say the visitors will tire of it; if so, it will be easy for those who do, to find most comfortable drawing, reading, smoking and billiard rooms out of its sound, and we must then console ourselves with the feeling that in our attempt to minister to the enjoyment of those who patronize the "Grand", we have gratuitously given them "too much of a good thing", an indiscretion that cannot be laid to the charge of many of the hotels we frequent.

Van Lier/Von Leer — the Dutch musician who took a German name but who changed it back in 1914.

In 1904 Herr Von Leer's contract was renewed and included the following conditions,

1. The Orchestra to be composed of five members viz:- himself as Musical Director, Mrs Flora Von Leer and three others to be selected by himself [Mrs Beatrix Sachs, daughter of the Von Leers, feels that her mother was an equally good violinist as her father and indeed before her marriage organised one of the first all-women orchestras, The Windsor Ladies Orchestra]. If any of the said performers should become indisposed or leave the Band he undertakes to replace them by musicians of equal skill.

2. The Orchestra to perform each day including Sunday for a further period from 17 October 1904 to 31 July 1905 at the following hours:-
   4.30 to 6 and 8.15 to 10 or such as may be arranged by the Manager.

3. Mr Von Leer and each member of the Orchestra to be granted one week's holiday during the said term. [No mandatory 4 week holidays in those days.]

4. Dances when required to be paid for at £1 per dance. [This means the whole orchestra receives £1 not that the participants pay £1.]

5. Payment £15.15.0 per week and £2.12.6 in lieu of food and refreshment of any description. [Out of this Von Leer had to pay his other musicians. Mrs Von Leer was a violinist too. Von Leer's brother, Jacques Van Lier was the famous cellist.]

By 1907 the success of the orchestra was such that the contract stipulated four others besides Mr and Mrs Von Leer and weekly remuneration had increased to £24 per week. The players were also allowed two weeks' holiday.

The Chairman had in fact praised the Von Leer orchestra in his address to shareholders at the end of 1904,

So highly do our visitors appreciate the music of Von Leer's orchestra that we have been induced, notwithstanding the depressed time and very heavy expense, to extend their engagement into the coming year. The excellence of their performance has met with enthusiastic appreciation, and compliments have frequently been bestowed on the Board for having had the courage to raise this department of our undertaking above the level of most hotels.

Herr Von Leer was not German but was in fact Van Lier, a Dutchman. He adopted the German name because it was considered at the time that the best musicians came from Germany. In 1914 for obvious reasons he changed it back to Van Lier.

CLAUDE DEBUSSY

We shall see more of Van Lier later but as he played at the Grand in 1905 there arrived a M. et Mme. Claude Debussy. The two guests, although they had been married, were not married to each other. The woman was in fact, Emma Bardac, Jewish wife of a prominent French financier, and she had enticed Debussy away from his simple seamstress wife, Rosalie. Rosalie had attempted to commit suicide but, in spite of the scandal, Debussy persisted with his affair with the elegant and wealthy Emma Bardac. Emma was sophisticated and an excellent singer and the impecunious Debussy fell for her.

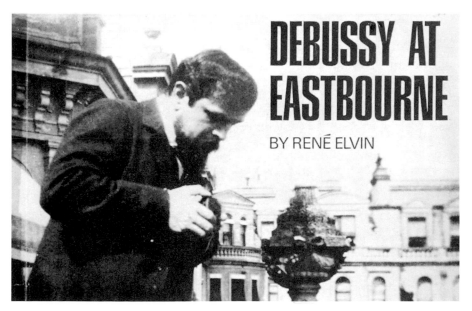

DEBUSSY AT EASTBOURNE

BY RENÉ ELVIN

Debussy at the Grand — "a peaceful and charming spot . . . relax like an animal".

When they arrived at the Grand Hotel, Emma was expecting his child. Indeed Debussy was effectively fleeing from the scandal and complications of his desertion. Whereas Emma had secured her divorce Debussy had funked appearing in court and was still married to Rosalie, or Lilly, as he called her. Debussy came to Eastbourne and to the Grand to relax which indeed he did writing to a friend that he found it "a peaceful and charming spot" where he could "relax like an animal."

The calm was broken by news reaching him of the judgement against him in the divorce suit brought by his wife and of the scathing comments of the Judge. This litigation, which continued, clearly upset Debussy who wrote to his friend, the music critic Louis Laloy, who became his first biographer,

> It would have been unpardonable to leave Paris without seeing you if my departure had not been a flight. I fled from all that tedious fuss. I fled from myself, who was finally only allowed to think by permission of the lawyers. I've been here a month. It's a little English seaside place, silly as these places sometimes are. I shall have to go because there are too many draughts and too much music — but I don't know quite where . . . I am trying somehow to get back to myself. I have written a certain amount of music, as I have not done for quite a time.

Whatever Debussy thought of Eastbourne, the draughts and the excess of music (you will remember the Chairman's comments on "too much of a good thing") he and Emma stayed for another month.

Mrs Sachs, the daughter of Van Lier, can remember her father saying that Debussy was very shy and was hardly ever seen in the public rooms. He went to the top gallery in the Hall and listened to a transcription of one of his piano arabesques, finally expressing himself very pleased with it.

Furthermore, while here he completed perhaps his greatest symphony — *La Mer*. In spite of later praise for the work, it was not initially well received in Paris. One of the critics remarked,

"I neither hear, nor see, nor feel the sea." Nevertheless it was later recognised as evocative of all the moods of the ocean.

It would not be fair to say that *La Mer*, although completed at Eastbourne, was inspired solely by the English Channel off the Sussex Coast. It had been formed over many years from reminiscences of many holidays by the sea. There is however some evidence to suggest that another of Debussy's famous pieces, *Reflets dans l'eau*, the first of his *Images pour piano*, was inspired by his watching the interplay of sun and cloud on an ornamental pool in Devonshire Park.

INCREASING NUMBERS

In the year that Debussy stayed at the Grand, 1905, the Chairman reported to the shareholders that the pressure of visitors was enormous. A Garage was added because of the

Eastbourne Pier in the early 1900s with the bath chair men waiting for custom.

increasing number of people who came in their cars or motors as they were called in those days. The Stillroom had to be enlarged and the Manager pointed out to the Board that on one of the crowded days of the "mid-term" at the schools (Eastbourne has many schools now but had many more then) the staff served 1,600 meals. On one of the days 354 sat down to lunch and on another 415 teas were provided. One of the shareholders was not surprised "when the visitors could listen to such lovely music".

By the end of 1907 the West Wing was functioning smoothly. The furnishing of the new suites as well as of the lounge and ballroom had been put in the hands of Maple and Co. and everyone seemed pleased with the results. The ballroom also boasted a sprung floor. The regrettable development of this year was the closure of the Tap or Bar near the Compton Street entrance. You will remember that this had operated as a concession but although it had brought £1,000 of profit the management were unhappy about the lack of control over the sale of all alcohol in the hotel.

TAXES AND DUTIES

As in the 1980s when company chairmen refer to the tax that the Chancellor of the Exchequer takes from us, so in 1911 Ernest Page talked of Lloyd George,

> Last year Mr Lloyd George, or one of his satellites, made a demand upon us for £534 for the extra licence duty. We made the best calculation that we could and came to the conclusion that it ought to be about £200. He would not have that, and insisted on having £534 as what was called an interim payment; but the result has been that the £534 has been not only enough for 1910, but also for the year 1911, and we have received back from the Government which, of

course, must have been great pain to that body of gentlemen, a cheque for £155.14s.2d.

Lloyd George also received some hard words about income tax at 1s 2d (about 6p) in the £ and about the higher rate of 1s 8d (about 8p) in the £.

In spite of such difficulties the hotel prospered and each year pushed up both turnover and profits until by 1912 the turnover had reached £90,000 (about £2 million in today's terms) with a net profit of £26,125 (about £520,000). The Chairman was able to speak jauntily about champagne,

> Champagne it is necessary to have and, if the Hotel is to give its customers the best, the champagne served must be vintage wines. As a fact, between the year 1906 and the year 1911 no vintage champagne has been brought upon the market, except to a very small extent some of 1907, and it became all important, having regard to the decreasing stock of vintage champagnes, and their greatly increasing price, that we should lay in an adequate supply, so as to have always on our Wine List abundant stocks of the best vintages until the vintage of 1911 is fit to be used. Therefore we, with no lavish hand invested in champagne, and I may say that the champagnes which are now in our cellar are today worth in the market, and could be sold by us and, if you think fit, shall be sold by us, for a great many hundreds of pounds more than we paid for them.

The ABC Railway Guide of 1908, perhaps the Egon Ronay guide of those days, spoke of

> electrical light in every room and lifts to all floors
> sanitary arrangements in the most modern and approved manner
> post, telegraph, telephone, chemist, hairdresser
> Turkish, Electric and Medical Baths
> Massage for both ladies and gentlemen
> experienced French chef
> table d'hôte and à la carte at separate tables
> terms moderate and no charge for attendance
> several self contained suites (comprising entrance lobby, sitting room and one or more bedrooms) recently added

separate suite, the Prince's Rooms, with private entrance suitable for
  receptions, wedding breakfasts, dinner
handsome Ballroom with private entrance with spring dancing floor
  on the latest improved principle
whole building warmed in winter
hotel omnibus meeting London trains
hiring of private carriages and horses
Motor Garage with pit

An etching of the hotel and gardens in the early 1900s.

It all typifies Edwardian elegance and leisure and all of these
luxuries could be enjoyed at these prices,

A single room	5s 6d (27.5p but really to keep pace with inflation 20−25 times that, i.e. £5.50−£6.00)
Full breakfast	3s (15p)
Table d'hôte lunch	3s (15p)

Cup of tea	6d (2.5p)
Full board	12s 6d (62.5p)

Even allowing for the depreciation of money the prices seem moderate but we must remember what people earned. We have already seen what the average working woman earned per week (11s 7d). In 1914 the average wage for the adult male industrial worker was £75 a year. There was an enormous gap between him and the average annual income of the salaried class of £340 per year, but even so neither of these classes was going to be able to afford the Grand even if they had thought of staying there which of course they would not have done in their wildest dreams.

The hotel omnibus calling at the railway station was the subject of an agreement drawn up between the hotel and the London Brighton and South Coast Railway (the railways were run by a series of regionalised private companies in those days). The language of the agreement is about as comprehensible as anything issued by the nationalised British Rail — perhaps when the Labour Government nationalised the railways in the 1940s they retained the same lawyers!

> The Company agrees to let and the Licensee agrees to take and accept the privilege of running a Motor propelled Omnibus (in common with others to whom the privilege shall or may be granted) to the Yard of the Eastbourne Railway Station belonging to the Company in the County of Sussex aforesaid for the exclusive convenience of the Visitors arriving for or departing from the said Hotel, for one quarter of the year from the twenty fourth day of June, One Thousand Nine Hundred and Eleven and thereafter until the said privilege shall be determined as hereinafter provided.

It was not however only the rich and privileged that the Grand tried to involve. A Mr Woodard, who still lives in Eastbourne, remembers the hotel's involvement in the local swimming baths. Indeed there was a Grand Hotel Swimming Club which held an annual swimming festival. In 1911 Mr Woodard, then a boy of six and a half, gave an exhibition of swimming and diving which was reported in the 'Reports' at the end of the year,

> It consisted of Swimming on Breast, Swimming on Back, Motionless, Floating, Arm Chair, Diving from Spring Board, Head Dive from 4th Step, Dummy Soldier Dive, Swallow Dive, Porpoise Dive, Diving through Hoop, His Idea of a Beginner's Dive, and concluded with High Dive. Some of the items gave a great deal of amusement, and the whole exhibition would be welcomed at a future festival. A special prize — a Biscuit Box — was presented to Master Woodard at the evening gathering.

Mr and Mrs Eeley, the manager and his wife, were of course present at the Festival.

The company was also gradually paying off its Debentures and indeed by 1912 was investing money in realisable stocks such as the Grand Trunk Railway of Canada. In the thirty years since the early 1880s turnover at the hotel had risen from £17,000 to £90,000. Dividends, partly in cash and partly in shares, had totalled £300,000 out of an income of £1,380,000.

To supervise this growth the directors took the following fees in 1911, 1912 and 1913

The Chairman	Mr Ernest Page	£580
	Mr Francis Burke	£285
	Mr Henry Gascoigne	£285
	Mr Samuel Eeley	£285

In addition as Manager, Sam Eeley received a salary of £750 and an annual bonus of £210. Mrs Eeley received £150 a year and a £105 bonus while John Cholmeley, the Secretary, received £450 plus a bonus of £78.15.0. Thus the Eeleys received in total £1,500 a year — not a king's ransom but still nearly four times the average salary and twenty times the average industrial wage.

The upper classes, their wives, their children and their

servants were coming to the hotel in increasing numbers. Herr Von Leer was entertaining them with his music, Mr and Mrs Eeley and their Head Waiter, Mr Gabb were looking after their every comfort. The tennis and croquet tournaments in Eastbourne were in full swing.

GUESTS OF THE GRAND

It is impossible to go into detail about all the Grand Hotel's impressive guests. The visitors' book reads like Debretts,

Lord Chancellor 1902

Lord and Lady Braye 1902

George and Percy and Sir Charles Wyndham 1902
Sir Charles Wyndham had fought in the American Civil War and had made his first theatrical appearance in America with John Wilkes Booth, the assassin of Abraham Lincoln. Sir Charles, by the time he stayed at the Grand, had built Wyndham's Theatre and was manager of the Criterion Theatre.

Lord Lytton 1902
Lord Lytton's daughter was a leading suffragette and suffered the full rigours of imprisonment where she was force-fed while on hunger strike in spite of a heart condition.

Lord and Mary Curzon 1904

Lord Kelvin 1905
Lord Kelvin, as William Thompson, invented the mirror galvanometer and siphon recorder in connection with submarine telegraphy, as well as the mariner's compass and navigation sounding machinery.

Lord Westminster 1906

Lord Abercorn 1906

The Rt. Hon. Sir Henry Campbell Bannerman (Prime Minister) 1907

Lord Selby (Speaker of the House of Commons) 1907

Lord Sheffield 1907
  Lord Sheffield took an English cricket eleven to Australia in the 1890s.

The Duke of Devonshire 1910

Lord Willingdon 1910
  Lord Willingdon, an MP for Hastings from 1900 to 1906 and for Bodmin from 1906 to 1910, became Governor of Bombay in 1913 and of Madras in 1919. He attended the League of Nations as the delegate for India in 1924 and became Governor General of Canada in 1926 before concluding a brilliant diplomatic career as Viceroy and Governor General of India from 1931 to 1936.

Count Togo (Prime Minister of Japan) 1911

Lord Greville

Margaret, Princess Frederick Charles of Hesse and Princess of Prussia 1913

Maximilian — Prinz von Hessen and 4 children 1913

King Constantine of Greece
  and Sophie, Queen of Greece 1913
  (they abdicated the following year)

Sir Ernest Shackleton 1914
  Sir Ernest had been a third lieutenant on the National Antarctic Expedition in 1901 and Commander of the British Antarctic Expedition in 1907. He was to be Commander again of the British Antarctic Expedition in 1914 shortly after his visit to the Grand. Later he was Director of the Equipment and Transport Mobile Forces in the North Russia campaign of 1918/9 and Commander of the British Oceanographical and Sub-Antarctic Expedition in 1921.

The Prince of Wales — from battleship HMS Collingwood

George Robey

Gustave Hamel
  (the German air ace of the First World War)

Maxwell Aitken (later Lord Beaverbrook) also came straight to the Grand when his ship from Canada docked at Southampton in 1912. Aitken had already made himself a rich man in Canada

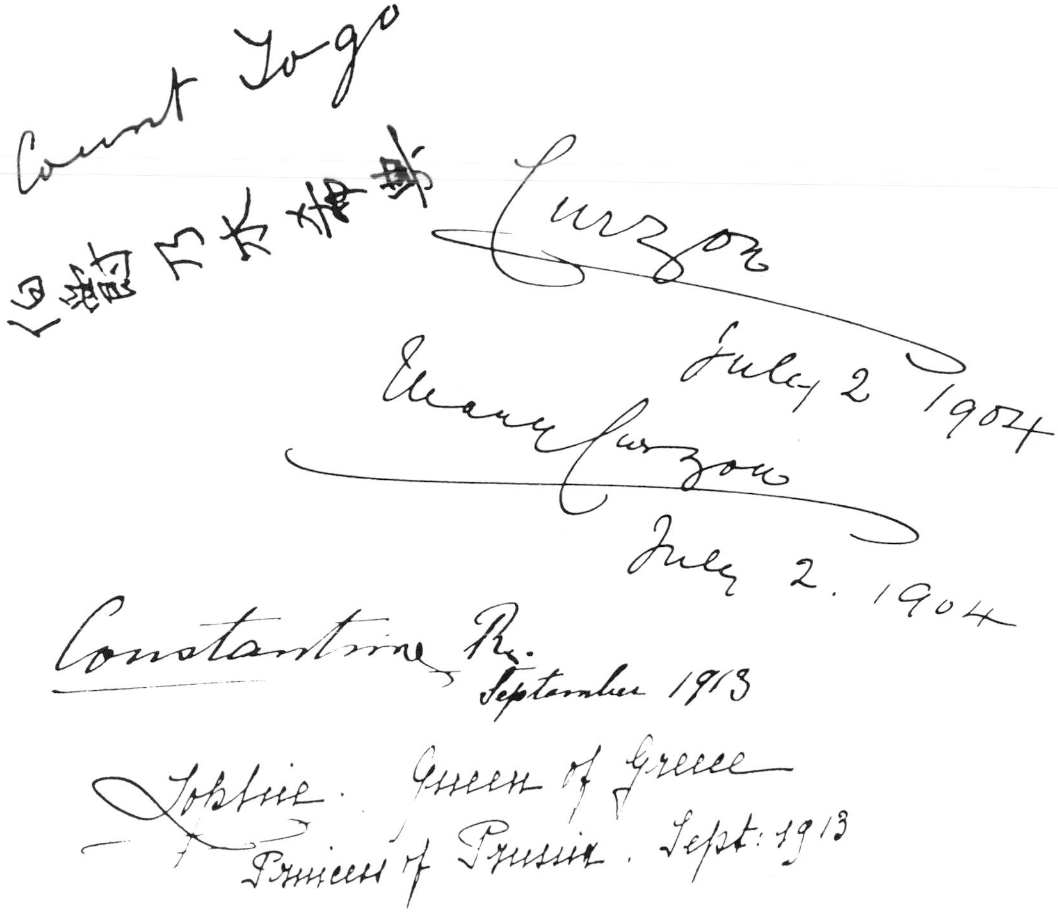

Count Togo

東郷平八郎

Curzon

July 2 1904

Mary Curzon

July 2. 1904

Constantine R.
September 1913

Sophie. Queen of Greece
Princess of Prussia. Sept: 1913

by promoting companies for public flotation. In some cases these had been overcapitalised and Aitken had received considerable criticism from irate shareholders who saw the value of their investments fall. He never in fact felt able to return to Canada but as we know he built himself a successful newspaper empire here and was even put in charge of production for the war effort in the Second World War by Winston Churchill.

Perhaps we could trace the history of the Curzons to give a flavour of the guests that the hotel entertained.

Lord Beaverbrook — the Grand was a safe haven after his arduous journey from Canada. (Photograph by courtesy of the BBC Hulton Picture Library.)

LORD AND MARY CURZON

Lord Curzon, descended from one of William the Conqueror's knights, became Viceroy of India in 1899. He married Mary, a determined American, and once they were installed in India they ruled almost as independent potentates. They entertained on a lavish scale. In each winter season they would give two levees, a Drawing Room, a State Ball, a State Evening Party, a Garden Party, several lesser balls, a number of official dinners as well as an informal dance and two or three smaller dinners every week. There would be 1,600 guests at the State Ball, 600 at each of the lesser balls, 120 at the large dinners and 1,500 at the State Evening Party which was mainly for Indians who did not dance. The most spectacular Government House function of Curzon's reign was the fancy dress ball of January 1903 at which the costumes were meant to recreate Wellesley's famous ball of 100 years before.

All this was too much for Mary who was very beautiful but also very fragile. Curzon's five-year term ended in 1904 and he returned to England with Mary where she became ill with peritonitis and almost died. The Curzons came to the Grand

Lord and Mary Curzon — an "eighteenth century" aristocrat with his beautiful American wife. (Photograph by courtesy of the BBC Hulton Picture Library.)

for Mary to recuperate before Curzon returned to his duties in India.

As we have already seen the hotel had been redecorated. Mr George Bagshawe, who lives in Carlisle, remembers visiting the Grand in the summers of 1910, 1911, 1912 and 1913,

It certainly was a *Grand* hotel in those days. In the evening the hotel porters were dressed in livery with white wigs, knee breeches and silk stockings. The Palm Court had a famous quartet orchestra conducted by a German Von Leer who played the violin [Mr Van Lier's pretending to be a German was obviously a successful marketing ploy] and other players on piano, double bass and cello. There was a huge stewards room for the chauffeurs, valets and ladies' maids, and another room for nannies and small children. The Head Waiter, a very imposing figure, was Mr Gabb. Everyone changed into evening dress for dinner every night and full evening dress (tail-coat) for Saturdays when there was a special concert by the orchestra.

I have the very happiest recollection of those really happy holidays.

Was there a cloud on the horizon? Yes — WAR!

CHAPTER THREE

THE WAR TO END ALL WARS

THE GREAT WAR, THE KAISER'S WAR

There can never have been a more appalling war where millions of men slogged it out for four solid years almost hand to hand in trenches. The best of the young men of Germany, France, Great Britain and her Empire and Dominions, Russia, Italy, and finally and therefore to a lesser extent, the United States were lost leaving in some cases their countries enfeebled and ripe for takeover by dictators and therefore for another great war.

It did change this country and many other countries. Lord Grey was prophetic when he said in August 1914 "The lights are going out all over Europe. They will not be lit again in our lifetime." Customs changed, people's horizons were broadened and even the leisured classes of the Victorian and Edwardian eras were affected. Indeed the young men of those classes were often the first into the recruiting offices. And yet, though scarcely a family was untouched by bereavement and in many all of the men were lost, it was not quite total war for the whole population as was the Second World War. Conscription did not arrive until 1916 and only 1917 and 1918 brought shortages and some rigid state control. For some time into the war the supply of munitions and the materials of war were left to private enterprise. The shortages and therefore thousands of deaths this caused eventually brought down Asquith's government in favour of that scourge of the laissez-faire businessman, Lloyd George. From then on the whole war effort became more national.

Draft leaving for the front — the town may not have suffered physically in the First World War but every family in the land was affected by personal loss.

EASTBOURNE IN THE WAR

Eastbourne did not suffer in the First World war as it was going to in the Second. Nevertheless it was not unscathed. John Stephens, who worked for many years in local government, can remember that the workhouse was cleared to make way for the army including an army hospital. He can still hear the bands accompanying the dead in their coffins on their way to the railway station or to Ocklynge Cemetery. John was also responsible for naming Fitzgerald Close after Lieutenant Colonel Oswald Fitzgerald who was aide-de-camp to Kitchener. When Kitchener's ship was sunk off the Outer Hebrides and the bodies were washed up on the shore most were unrecognisable but Fitzgerald's was identified and was brought back and buried in Eastbourne after a funeral at All Saints Church.

THE GRAND HOTEL AND THE KAISER'S WAR

Whatever the horrors of the war at the Front, in fact because of the horrors of the war at the Front, havens of peace and luxury like the Grand Hotel were important to those that could afford them. The painter Paul Nash summed up the horror in a letter to his wife,

> The rain drives on, the stinking mud becomes more evilly yellow, the shell-holes fill up with green-white water, the roads and tracks are covered in inches of slime, the black dying trees ooze and sweat and the shells never cease. They alone plunge overhead, tearing away the rotting tree stumps, breaking the plank roads, striking down horses and mules, annihilating, maiming, maddening, they plunge into the grave which is this land; one huge grave, and cast up on it the poor dead. It is unspeakable, godless, hopeless.

The war-weary needed a rest from that and the Grand tried to give it to them.

THE VIEW OF A PAGE BOY AND WAITER

Programmes of Van Lier/Von Leer music. By 1916 Germans, Bulgarians, Turks and Armenians were definitely not acceptable.

For all that, the most immediate effect of the outbreak of war was a shortage of waiters, not because all the English ones joined up, but because many of them were German and they naturally fled back to Germany. A Mr E. Dury, who lives at Warwick, has reason to remember the German waiters leaving for it brought him promotion from page boy to waiter. His memories bring us a view of the hotel from a lowly level,

Left school 1913. Mother was a widow in service. A Mr Gabb who was a butcher in Minchinhampton, Gloucestershire, was a relation to

Mr Gabb at the Grand Hotel, so I was taken on. To go to work at the hotel one had to have all one's underclothes with your name on as washing was done by hotel laundry. My first job was in the plate room under a Mr Swaldling to get used to things. I slept in the ground floor basement of the East Wing. Our first job was to empty and clean ashtrays in the lounge. Then breakfast. Sometimes Mr Gabb would inspect us while having breakfast for tidyness and clean hands. As a page boy we delivered letters to room floors and letters handed to visitors were on a silver tray with respect.

There were three lifts — East Wing, West Wing and Centre, which was hydraulic. Sometimes when the lift-man was off duty, one had to operate the hydraulic lift, which was a bit dodgy, for you had to pull the rope to stop and start. The others were electric. As a page boy I once tried on a lady's dress and was reported to Mr Gabb who sent me into the plate room for a week. As a waiter, I had to learn how to wait at table, pour wine, fold napkins. Finger bowls were laid on tables with a slice of lemon in them.

Mr Dury also remembers that a wealthy jeweller from Regent Street in London stayed at the hotel and would send a page boy with sealed parcels to post. The page boy went on a bicycle. As Mr Dury put in, "He would not dare to do it in this day and age."

Mr Dury also remembers delivering a letter to an Austrian lady with a lovely daughter. She was singing the song, 'A little love, a little kiss'. Her daughter told her not to sing that song as it was common. Common or not, it became a great hit during the War.

Mr Dury remembers the housekeeper, Miss Houston, as very strict and "you had to behave when upstairs". He remembers bathrooms on each floor but also that hot water was taken to the rooms each morning by the chambermaids.

When he was off duty Mr Dury used to go on boat trips on the steam ship, *Brighton Queen* to Hastings for 1s 6d (7.5p), returning by train. He also used to go up to Beachy Head and have tea at a small hut there. He would cycle to Polegate and listen to the military band on the Parade. His main pleasure was swimming in the Devonshire Park Baths.

Mr Dury likes to quote from Kipling when he thinks of his days at the Grand, "Walk with kings but do not lose the common touch".

While Mr Dury was getting on with his job as page boy and then waiter, the war was of course beginning to have an effect on business at the hotel. War was finally declared on 4 August 1914 though there had been strong rumblings for several weeks. This of course was in the height of the season and the immediate effect was,

> to drive people away from the sea, to hinder them from coming to the sea, and to establish a feeling of insecurity with regard to the safety of our coast towns.

This initial panic soon subsided and things returned to normal except that people felt obliged to spend less and save more. In a high overhead business like a hotel, those extra pounds are essential to profitability and by November 1914, the Chairman was warning the shareholders of hard times to come as long as the war lasted. But he was also confident of survival until better times arrived,

> We have a large sum of money to play with, and the receipts must fall to an even greater extent than they have fallen at the present time before the condition of things will be so altered as to make it necessary for the Directors substantially to reduce the dividend of our Company. I think we may pride ourselves on this fact: that probably of all the hotels in the United Kingdom the Grand Hotel, Eastbourne, has suffered and is continuing to suffer less from the War than any other. How that comes about is due, I suppose, to the popularity which we have gained and which I cannot help thinking we have deserved (Hear, hear). While other great establishments which I know of have been deserted by their clients to an extra-ordinary extent, we even now on many occasions are quite full and always have a very fair showing of guests.

Mr Page also boasted in this report of the new kitchens. He admitted that the old kitchen was not quite worthy of the Grand but was confident that Mr Eeley could now take guests into the kitchen, as apparently he was often asked to do, and they would find it,

> so delightful, so clean, so airy, so generally appetising, that I am sure they will go back to their friends and tell them: 'If you go to the Grand Hotel, Eastbourne, you will find a place where food is supplied to you which is cooked under the best conditions.'

As a gesture to the war, and also perhaps because of the benefit to cash-flow, the company decided to deduct income tax from the dividends before payment. As income tax rose because of the war this proved to be a wise move. The company also felt obliged to make redundant or "clear out" as Mr Page put it in his report to shareholders all German and Austrian waiters, whether naturalised or not. Mr Page regretted this as many had English wives and children and also because it brought great strain on the dining room. Suitable English waiters were not easily found and certainly not quickly. Mr Gabb's work in these difficult times was recognised by the Board and he was promoted from Head Waiter to Superintendent of the Hotel, immediately under Mr Eeley.

Although Ernest Page had anticipated a decline in receipts and profit, the year to September 1915 in fact brought an increase in both. The rate of inflation was, of course, starting to increase as it always does in time of war, but nevertheless it was a very satisfactory result. The Board even recommended an increase in dividend from 12 to 13%. One interesting point was that even in 1915 an insurance policy was taken out against damage from enemy air-raids. It cost £246 6s 7d. (perhaps the equivalent of £5,000 today).

And so it continued. Receipts and profits were up in 1916 and the dividend was increased again to 14%. Ernest Page became euphoric, here today it becomes quite natural to look back ten years, because it is exactly ten years ago since Mr & Mrs Eeley first came to us at Eastbourne and it is only just a little more than ten years since I first became a director of the Company. I have therefore ventured to compare the accounts of the year 1916 with those of the year 1906 … I find that in the year 1906 the hotel receipts were £53,488. In the year 1916 they are £106,821, and most of you must be mathematicians enough to see they have exactly doubled (Mr Page would probably have been flattered if described as patronising and pompous). The net profit in 1906 was £11,847; last year it was £24,541, an increase of 107 per cent.

The Reserves in 1906 were £54,981; they are now £100,013, which is an increase of 82 per cent, and I may say that the increase would have been 117 but for the fact that in the course of the ten years we gave the shareholders a bonus in shares of £19,656. Ten years ago we had mortgages to the extent of £7,000. They have all been paid off. Ten years ago the Debentures were £75,000. They are now only £65,000, etc. etc. Gentlemen, I think the comparisons which I have made between those two years, the first and last of the decade, show that the progress of the property of the Hotel Company has been little short of marvellous.

We will not be suprised to learn that after all this progress the directors accepted an increase in their fees from £1,750 to £2,250. It was perhaps unfortunate that in the whole of the 19 pages of Report of the General Meeting of 1916 it was not possible to mention the sacrifices being made in the war at the Front. It was after all the year when losses became so great that conscription was introduced, first for unmarried men (January) and then for married men (May). Not even the employees of the Grand who were called up were mentioned.

The war continued to be good news for the hotel. In 1917 receipts and profits increased again and the dividend was also increased to 16%. The staff did now receive a mention. In fact 200 had joined up and it was proposed that £1,000 should be allocated to those who had suffered because of the war. Twenty were known to have been killed and seven or eight were known to be missing while others had been taken prisoner. Ernest Page was quite open about the fact that the hotel was profiting out of the war,

> So far as the finances of the Company are concerned, we have gained by the War.

Insurance against attack from the air was still thought necessary and the company now felt it was time to be covered against bombardment from the sea as well.

Those lucky enough to visit the Grand still found the good things of life there. A menu of 17 January 1917 offered,

"Huitres Nature"

followed by

"Tortue Claire"

followed by

"Filets de Sole à la Grenobloise"

followed by

"Tournedos garnis Bouquetière" with
"Chouxfleurs Beurre fondu"

followed by

"Scotch Woodcock"

Better than bullybeef and rats in the trenches!

Ernest Page goes on in his report to give us an insight into how he as a director viewed one of his employees,

> Among those of the staff who have joined the King's Forces, I should mention the name of one of our Secretaries, Mr Sidney H. Smith. He is doing his duty, and I believe he has now got a commission. I do not think he has yet been abroad, but no doubt he is going to one of the war centres, and I am quite sure that when that happens, he will not disgrace the Grand Hotel.

Incredibly the good news from the hotel continued as the war ground on and 1918 was a record year with receipts at £156,000, 50% higher than only two years before. Ernest Page was able to say,

> I do not think it would be a good thing if the earnings remained quite as large, because life is almost impossible for the servants at an hotel

when it is a perpetual hurry and scurry for 365 days, as it has been in the last year. Over and above that in war time people will stand almost anything. They cannot get a place to lay their heads in London, and therefore, however many they can get into a bedroom at Eastbourne, they are only too glad to come there for the purpose of finding some place where they can lie down.

Ernest Page went on to criticise the Excess Profits Tax which meant the shareholders were paying 10s (50p) in the pound instead of 5s 6d (27.5p) or 6s (30p).

That is not fair, and it cannot go on. It will stifle energy and it will stifle competition if it does.

(Mr Page is perhaps fortunate not to have survived to the peacetime 1970s when a Labour Government raised income tax on the highest incomes to 98%, or the 1980s where a free enterprise Conservative Government was constantly criticised for reducing the top rate of tax to 60p in the pound.) Be that as it may, the Dividend was raised yet again to 17% and shareholders received a one for four bonus issue of shares. The war had been dramatically good for business for the Grand and indeed for the Directors for the shareholders now approved an increase in their fees to £2,500 and an honorarium of £1,000 free of tax.

Mildred Carter, who later worked at the Grand Hotel, with her friends at the Eastbourne Airplane Company.

AFTER THE WAR

Even the first year of peace was a boom year for the hotel and receipts increased again by £17,000. Ernest Page had forecast a downturn which did not happen but he again forecast a downturn for 1920,

> you must not expect to receive the very large income which we have taken in the year which is under discussion. France is open, Switzerland is open, the East Coast which was shut up during the years of the war, is open. There are no Americans coming here, because they are not able to get shipping. People who have lived at the Grand Hotel in the winter months during the period of the war are now going to Monte Carlo, Mentone [sic] and so on, and the consequence is that there is not in fact the great rush to our Hotel that there was a year ago.

Mr Page suggested that comparisons should be made with pre-war days and assured the shareholders that in autumn 1919 they were doing better than in autumn 1913.

PROPERTY PURCHASES

The Board showed themselves to be very astute in the purchase of properties. In 1918 they bought 18 acres at Willingdon close to the golf links, plus two cottages for just £1,025 (you will see later at what price they were to sell this land in 1952 and can imagine what it might be worth today). To round this purchase off they paid £330 for another 4 acres. The plan was to make the hotel self-supporting in vegetables. In 1919 3,000 trees were planted — apples, plums and pears. 1919 was in fact a very dry year and the plans for laying out a market garden were temporarily thwarted by the lack of water either from heaven or artificially from below. This problem was solved at the end of 1919 by the company's securing an artificial water supply from

Eastbourne. Ernest Page was shrewd enough to realise the potential of the land,

> I hope that we shall find great advantage from the possession of this large property, which ultimately must become very beneficial to the Company, because it is so near Eastbourne and is such a splendid site for houses, that portions of it are pretty certain to be in demand before very long for the purpose of building.

By 1920 this garden and farm at Willingdon were prospering so well that up to the end of September 1920 40 tons of potatoes were raised worth £14 to £15 a ton. The land yielded 20,000 cabbages, 5,000 heads of celery, 5,000 cauliflowers, 2 tons of turnips, 2 tons of carrots and 2 tons of parsnips. In their first year the apple trees yielded 20 bushels of apples and in between the trees were planted 1,000 gooseberry bushes and 1,000 black currant and red currant bushes. The farm was also yielding two to three dozen eggs a day. By the end of 1920 the weekly yield from the farm would have cost £40 in the market. As the weekly wages were £15 to £20 it would seem that the farm was already profitable. (Mr Page was being a little simplistic in suggesting in his annual report that £40 a week meant £2,000 a year — surely the yield in January and February could hardly match that of August and September.) Sam Eeley was able to point out to his guests that the vegetables, fruit and eggs came from the hotel's own farm.

The company also bought a house in Grand Parade which formed part of the Mostyn Hotel, presumably to prevent an extension to that hotel. But most important they bought, quickly and without reference to the shareholders, a property next to the Burlingon Hotel on Grand Parade. It was a property of three acres with three houses and fine grounds. It had been advertised as,

> Affording an exceptional opportunity to capitalists, syndicalists and others for the erection of a first-class hotel with ample grounds.

In a masterly piece of understatement Ernest Page reported to his shareholders that,

> We thought it was much better that that place, which was to be sold for the erection of a first-class hotel with ample grounds, should be in our hands than anybody else's. (Hear, hear.) As a matter of fact, we decided to give, if necessary, very considerably in excess of the amount which ultimately we secured it for at auction; and I believe it is a fact that, even if there is no increase, which there will be, in the annual rent received from the property and which we get at the present moment, we shall receive in rent something like 4.5 per cent on our outlay, which is not so bad after all. Even if we were to get no rent at all, I should have been in favour of buying the place.

Pompous and patronising he may have been but Mr Ernest Page was also very shrewd.

The whole three acres plus the houses were bought for £25,000. This was indeed a bargain and when Sam Eeley went to visit the property and was telling the gardener that the Grand Hotel Company had bought it the gardener said,

> No, Sir, you have not bought it; it was guv yer.

VAN LIER LEAVES THE HOTEL

As the war period ended one of the assets of the hotel also departed. Van Lier received an offer from the London musical agents, Keith Prouse and left in the autumn of 1919. When Mrs Flora Van Lier left the hotel presented her with a beautiful emerald ring. Her daughter, Mrs Beatrix Sachs, still wears it.

Van Lier had set the musical standard for the Grand Hotel which was to become a watchword as the broadcasts of the 1920s took their music throughout the country and indeed, throughout the world. During Van Lier's time at the Grand the hotel had been graced with visits from many of the greatest musicians of the day.

S. VAN LIER

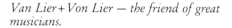

Van Lier + Von Lier — the friend of great musicians.

The Belgian violinist, conductor and composer Eugene Ysaye came. Carl Flesch said of Ysaye "he was the most outstanding violinist I have ever heard in my life" and this was an opinion shared by a generation of violinists — Kreisler, Thibaud, Szigeti and Enesco. Ysaye was the pioneer of twentieth-century violin playing. He died in 1931 but in 1937 the Concours International Eugene Ysaye (now known as the Queen Elisabeth competition) was instituted. Its first winner was David Oistrakh.

Another famous visitor was the Czech violinist and composer, Jan Kubelik who was acclaimed by many as a second Paganini. His technical mastery was complete and he was of course father of the conductor and composer, Rafael Kubelik, for some years permanent conductor at the Royal Opera House, Covent Garden.

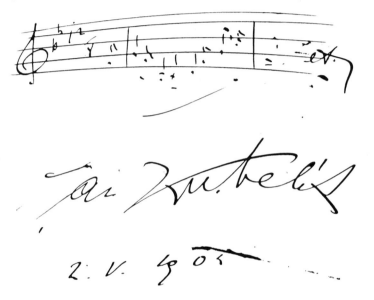

Also from Europe to meet Van Lier there came Jan Paderewski, the pianist, composer and statesman from Poland. After a slow start to his career Paderewski became a great favourite in both Britain and America receiving many honorary doctorates — first Lvov in his own country, and then Yale, Krakow, Oxford, Columbia, Southern California, Poznan, Glasgow and Cambridge. He turned to politics in mid-life and became Prime Minister and Minister of Foreign Affairs in the new independent Poland of 1919. He signed the notorious Treaty of Versailles as his country's representative. After the Nazis invaded Poland in 1939 he went on a large fund-raising tour in the United States and when he died in 1940 he was afforded a state funeral in Arlington National Cemetery.

[signature: J. Paderewski]

A pupil of Paderewski, the Anglo-American pianist Harold Bauer also came to the Grand. Originally a violinist Paderewski advised him to switch to the piano and Bauer established a fine reputation both in Britain, where he introduced Debussy's works to British audiences, and in America where he founded the Beethoven Association of New York, the most important organisation for the performance of chamber music in New York between the wars.

Then there was Jean Gerardy, the Belgian 'cellist who had first performed in Britain at a concert in Nottingham in which Ysaye and Paderewski also took part, and the intensely individual Fritz Kreisler, the Austrian who had won the Premier Grand Prix de Rome at the age of 12 against 40 competitors who were all at least 20 years of age. Kreisler went on to perform the Elgar violin concerto, dedicated to him, for the first time in London, St Petersburg, Moscow, Vienna, Berlin, Dresden, Munich and Amsterdam.

From Italy came Paolo Tosti, composer of so many famous songs — 'Forever', 'Goodbye', 'Mother', 'At Vespers', 'Armore', 'Aprile', 'Vorrei Morire' and 'That Day'. Also from

Italy came perhaps the greatest tenor of all time, Enrico Caruso, whose combination of power and sweetness of voice and whose breath control were unequalled. In 1902 he had joined with Nellie Melba in Puccini's *La Bohème* at Monte Carlo which launched his brilliant career, but perhaps the performance which established above all others his fame was his Rudolfo in *La Bohème* at Covent Garden in 1904.

A cartoon of himself by Caruso, perhaps the greatest tenor of all time.

Then of course there was the unique Dame Nellie Melba. Born in Melbourne as Helen Mitchell, the daughter of a Scot, Nellie was already singing in a concert at Richmond (Melbourne) Town Hall at the age of 6. She came to London in 1886 and after one concert went to Paris to study under Mathilde Marchesi. After 12 months her teacher pronounced her ready and she made her debut in 1887 as Gilda in Verdi's *Rigoletto* at the Théâtre de la Monnaie, Brussels. She appeared under the name Melba, presumably derived from her native Melbourne. She was an instantaneous success and was immediately engaged by Harris for his season of Italian opera at Covent Garden in 1888. She went on to many triumphs throughout the world over the next forty years where audiences thrilled to her silvery tone with its bright "girlish" quality and her remarkable evenness across a compass of two and a half octaves. She became, of course, a great favourite of Edward VII and sang for him and Queen Alexandra at Buckingham Palace for the entertainment of Archduke Franz Ferdinand of Austria. She was made a Dame Commander of the British Empire and continued to give concerts until 1926 when she was 67.

Nellie Melba
Feb 25th 1926

The date of my
farewell appearance
in Eastbourne

PÊCHE MELBA

Today the name melba means either a piece of thin toast or a dessert. The toast was not in fact named after Nellie though she did like thin toast. On the other hand "Pêche Melba" certainly was created for her and many chefs claimed to be the creator.

The true creator was the great Auguste Escoffier, head chef at the Savoy under Cesar Ritz at the turn of the century. Melba sent Escoffier two orchestra seats for a Covent Garden performance of Lohengrin in which she appeared with Jean de Reszke. The next day at a supper party Melba gave for the Duc d'Orleans Escoffier prepared the dessert in a large silver cup placed between the wings of a swan — the *Lohengrin* swan — made of ice. The true recipe according to Escoffier's own cookbook, the world famous *Guide Culinaire* is,

> After peeling the peaches, poach them in vanilla flavoured syrup. Put them in a timbale upon a layer of vanilla ice cream, and coat them with a raspberry puree.

That, of course, is exactly how you would have Pêche Melba at the Grand. It is in stark contrast to the tinned peaches, glob of ice cream and sickly syrup we all receive at most establishments.

Nellie Melba — "After peeling the peaches, poach them in vanilla flavoured syrup . . .'
(Photograph by courtesy of the BBC Hulton Picture Library.)

PAVLOVA

Another supreme artist who came to the Grand Hotel (and one who also lives on today on menus throughout the world) was the Russian Anna Pavlova, perhaps the greatest ballerina of all time. Pavlova appeared on most of the famous stages of the world and with most of the great dancers of her time — Mordkin, Novikoff and Volinine of the Imperial Ballet of

Moscow; Fokine, Bolm, Nijinsky and Vladimiroff of her own St Petersburg Academy. She received more homage than almost anyone else in the world of theatre before or since.

Anna Pavlova — the beautiful Russian ballerina.
(Photograph by courtesy of the BBC Hulton Picture Library.)

Of the famous English musicians who came there was the conductor and composer Sir Landon (actual name Russell) Ronald (we shall see later how Tom Jones used to tease him) and Myra Hess who was later to be made a Dame for her organisation of midday chamber concerts at the National Gallery during the Second World War. That most famous of

[Handwritten note:] my very kindest regards to Mr & Mrs Van Leer

Myra Hess.

Andante

Eastbourne 24th August 1911

conductors, Sir Henry Wood, also came. As we know we now have the Sir Henry Wood Promenade Concerts, a fitting tribute to the man who organised so many works at the Queen's Hall. Richard Strauss, Debussy, Reger, Skrabin and Schoenburg all visited London to conduct for him or hear him conduct their works. And then of course there was Sir Thomas Beecham, the conductor responsible above all others for spreading the playing and enjoyment of orchestral music to all corners of the British Isles. He improved the standard of British orchestras and introduced works previously little known, especially those of Debussy, Strauss, Stravinsky and Berlioz. He was the initiator and maintainer of the Mozart cult.

Finally of the Englishmen we have that great and prolific composer, Sir Edward Elgar. His style may have owed much to Wagner but he was the truly British composer who wrote, as in *Pomp and Circumstance*, what the British wanted to hear. The British had found a new Handel but this man was English born and bred. He composed a huge number of works for stage, for church for choirs with orchestra and unaccompanied, for orchestra, for organ, for chamber music, for violin, for piano and for songs.

This roll call of famous musicians who came to the Grand would not be complete without mentioning the two Russians, Chaliapin and Vladimir de Pachmann. Chaliapin blended both vocal and dramatic genius while the pianist Pachmann set him-

Sir Henry Wood — the organiser of so many works in the Queen's Hall.

Sir Thomas Beecham — spread music to all corners of the British Isles.

self such a high standard that he would stop in the middle of a performance and say to his audience, "Ah, that was not true Pachmann" and play the piece again.

The Board were determined to replace Van Lier with someone of equal talent and were able to secure Arthur Beckwith as the new leader of the Orchestra. Beckwith had been a gold medallist at the Royal College of Music and also first violin to Sir Henry Wood at the Queen's Hall. Mr Page told shareholders in his best pompous strain,

> I happened to be at the Grand the first night he came, and I can truly say that after he had finished his violin solo I have never heard at any period of the Hotel's existence so much enthusiasm as was expressed all round by the guests. He will do, gentlemen. He will draw visitors to the Hotel, and he will maintain our musical pre-eminence.

THE APPOINTMENT TO THE BOARD
OF CECIL GRANTHAM PAGE ————————————

The end of the war also brought the death of one of the directors, Henry Gascoigne, and he was replaced by Ernest Page's son, Cecil Page. He was, like his father, a member of the Bar. He had volunteered in October 1914 and was wounded or as his father put it,

> he is here now, I am glad to say, pretty nearly sound, although he still suffers, and always will suffer to some extent, from the effects of a Hun bullet.

Cecil Page worked in the office of Sir Albert Stanley which controlled the Underground and all the buses in London. He was a young man and clearly destined to become Chairman of the Company.

Sir Edward Elgar — wrote what the British wanted to hear.

CHAPTER FOUR

"I AM NOW TAKING YOU OVER TO THE GRAND HOTEL, EASTBOURNE"

BRITAIN IN THE 1920s

The Kaiser's War was of course a cataclysmic event but in terms of society it did not bring the changes that its successor, Hitler's War, was to bring, nor did it bring to Britain the political and economic turmoil that occurred in continental Europe. There were no occupation forces as there were in Germany and no actual bank closures (though for many of the population there might as well have been for they had no money to lose). There was no runaway inflation. Indeed, after the sharp inflation of the immediate post-war boom there was an initial sharp fall in prices and a continual gradual decline right through to 1939.

WORKING CLASS MILITANCY

There had been a great deal of industrial unrest in the years leading up to the war when prices had been rising faster than wages. Now, after four years of grind and slaughter, the working class had been promised "a land fit for heros", and they were not happy with the reality of sharply rising unemployment and threatened wage cuts. Parts of the country and indeed many in government and the ruling classes expected revolution. Lloyd George, by then Prime Minister, expressed his fears to his colleagues,

> they could not take risks with labour. If we did, we should at once create an enemy within our own borders, and one which would be better provided with dangerous weapons than Germany. We had in this country millions of men who had been trained to arms, and there were plenty of guns and ammunition available.

His fears of wholesale revolution were almost certainly unfounded but nevertheless there was a great deal of industrial unrest. Even during the war there had been short police strikes and in August 1919 they broke out again in London and Liverpool. This led to extensive rioting and looting in Liverpool and the government sent in 2,600 troops, four tanks, while a battleship, HMS *Valiant* and two destroyers stood off the port. A civilian died after a volley of shots and bayonet charges were ordered on the Saturday night.

The miners and railwaymen went on strike to resist the owners' attempts to cut wages. They joined the General Workers in the famous Triple Alliance. (The General Council of the TUC was only formed in 1920.) In April 1921 the government declared a state of emergency under the Emergency Powers Act which had been passed in October 1920 and prepared to call up the army reserve. Lloyd George announced that,

> the country is facing a situation analagous to civil war.

In the event the other two parties of the Triple Alliance deserted the miners as they were to do again in 1926 and negotiated settlements were reached — in most cases they meant a reduction in wages.

THE BRITISH INSTITUTIONS
STAND FIRM ————————————————————

Amidst this labour unrest and deteriorating economic conditions how were the other classes faring? The basic British institutions remained untouched. The middle class went about their business and the new technologies gradually brought the chance for a few to be upwardly mobile. The upper classes still dominated finance, politics and industry and many behaved as though the war had been an unpleasant interruption to the life they had led in the Victorian era.

Arthur Marwick in his excellent book, *Britain in Our Century* illustrates how the Board of the newly formed Imperial Chemical Industries (ICI) combined all the elements of the ruling class. There was

> Rufus Isaacs, 1st Marquess of Reading, who had been Lord Chief Justice, and then for five years, Viceroy of India (his son, incidentally, had married Alfred Mond's daughter Eva), Lord Birkenhead (the former F.E. Smith, successively in the 1920s Lord Chancellor and Secretary for India), Lord Weir, the Scottish shipping magnate and pillar of Toryism, and Sir John Anderson, permanent Under Secretary at the Home Office, and director of the government's preparations against the General Strike; the first Treasurer was recruited from the Inland Revenue. Sir Alfred Mond (the first Chairman) himself shortly became Lord Melchett.

THERE WERE CHANGES ————————————————

Thus, the classes were very much in place as before. For the working class employment meant hard physical labour for very poor wages and the constant threat of unemployment or at least a reduction in wages. There was a lower middle class of shopkeepers and white collar workers and an upper middle class of lesser businessmen, managers and professionals. There was an upper class of titled and still mostly landed families with their partners those in government and at the very top of finance and business. The educational system perpetuated this structure — expensive and prestigious public schools for the upper middle classes, grammar schools for the lower middle classes and elementary schools for the working class.

But changes were coming to create a few ripples on this stagnant pond. Women had advanced a great deal since the Edwardian era. The country had needed them during the war and both the country and they themselves now realised they were capable of tasks never before considered. They won the vote for women over 30 in 1919 and for all women over 21 in 1928. There were of course many more young women than young men in the 1920s because of the slaughter of the war and the so-called "Flapper" appeared on the scene. She smoked, applied make-up in public, showed her legs and did the new-fangled American dance, the Charleston.

A parade of young ladies — the shortage of young men after the Great War meant that ladies became a little more forward in the 1920s. (Photograph by courtesy of the BBC Hulton Picture Library.)

The motor car, a play-thing of the rich before the war, and still not conceivable for the working class, was now within reach of many in the middle classes. In 1922 there were 952,000 on the roads. By 1930 it was 2,218,000. This meant that 20% of families owned one. As we shall see the motor car had its effect on the business of the Grand Hotel.

Another innovation, with a much greater effect on the Grand, was the radio or wireless. The British Broadcasting Corporation was set up in October 1922 and in December 1922 John (later Lord) Reith took over as General Manager. Initially the radio too remained an upper and middle class phenomenon — there were only two million licences by 1930.

Changes then were occurring and by the end of the 1920s with a Labour Party in power the Government was trying to realise some of the aspirations of the people. In the event world economic crisis was to thwart them, plunging the country into the worst depression in living memory.

How did the Grand Hotel fare in this world of change but no change?

THE GRAND HOTEL IN THE 1920s — PROFITS

The 1920s was still a prosperous era for the Grand Hotel. The hotel had built itself an enviable reputation and as we have seen had enjoyed a successful war. It had made a lot of money and was extremely soundly based in financial terms.

1921 in fact brought a downturn in receipts from £168,000 to £151,000 though the corresponding decline in profit was only £1,906. The decline in receipts was blamed by the Chairman on competition from resorts both on the Continent and also on the East Coast. He also blamed the Coal Strike (mentioned above) which caused great disruption to the railway service between London and Eastbourne.

The Grand Hotel football team 1920—1. The hotel ran many sports teams and actively encouraged participation.

1922 brought a further decline in receipts of £9,400 and again a lesser decline in profits of £1,237. This time the blame fell on,

The fact is we find at Eastbourne, as people find elsewhere, that the ordinary Britisher is by no means so well off as he was just after the war came to an end.

The people were coming to the Grand in large numbers but were not spending as much as they had done. Nevertheless the Board felt able to recommend a bonus issue of one share for every five held.

After a small upturn in 1923, 1924 saw another fall of £8,500 in receipts with a fall of £3,500 in profits. The blame this time fell squarely on the weather,

> The execrable weather. I suppose 1924 was about the worst year there has been for the last fifty years.

(It is perhaps reassuring to read such comments as we all imagine that in our youth, and certainly in the youths of our parents and grandparents, the sun shone all the time.)

Strangely, Ernest Page, still the Chairman of the Grand Hotel, Eastbourne Limited, also blamed the Wembley Exhibition. Wembley Stadium had recently been built (football aficionados will know, of course, that the first F.A. Cup Final was played there in 1923 and most of us will have seen the photographs of the police trying to control the crowds who tried to get in to that first final), and a large exhibition was held there in the summer of 1924. This had been expected to benefit the resorts of Eastbourne, Folkestone, Brighton and Bournemouth with visitors from the USA and Europe. It did not.

1925 brought some excitement at the Annual General Meeting. It began quietly and auspiciously enough with the Chairman congratulating himself and his Board on the splendid deal they had done selling off the Victoria Estate Property at a profit of £10,484. This was the property they had bought in 1919 next to the Sussex Club consisting of the three large houses — Rosemount, Norfolk Lodge and Pine Grange. You will remember that they bought it to prevent it being turned into another luxury hotel.

Ernest Page had congratulated himself at the time for buying it for £25,000 and he did so again now. He went on to remind shareholders that he had sold the Sussex Club to the Duke of Devonshire for £6,000 with the proviso that it should remain a club and if the Duke or his descendants ever wanted to sell it the Grand Hotel would have the option of buying it back for

£6,500. As Page now pointed out the other three properties could never be a threat as a hotel without the Sussex Club because that was the only property with sea frontage. The Board had therefore sold the other three properties for £32,500 leaving a profit of £10,484 13s 4d on the whole deal. "Hear, hear" was heard and a shareholder, Mr Weldon, rose to congratulate the Board and propose that an honorarium of 1,000 guineas free of all taxation should be given to the Board in recognition of their services in the purchase and sale of these properties.

I move that resolution, and I trust that it will be seconded.

To the surprise and dismay of all a Mrs Vickers rose and instead of seconding the motion launched an attack on the Board. (In view of what has been said about the position of women in society it is interesting that the first dissenting voice in 40 years of resolutions at annual meetings should be a female one.)

I have heard such praise of your Directors, and I am quite certain that they do everything for us that they can. But the fact remains, however, that the receipts from the hotel business are less than they were in 1923. The Profit and Loss Account also shows that the net profit for the year, though better than for 1924, is still considerably less than it was in 1923 and the preceding years. Notwithstanding that, the Directors are receiving fees exceeding one-tenth of the whole net profits of the Company. These are the facts that have led me to protest against this extra remuneration, and if this resolution goes to a vote I shall consider it my duty to demand a poll.

A Mr Holman then rose and made a long speech commending the Board, their astuteness and alertness and finally seconding the motion. Ernest Page, totally unused to any opposition, asked,

Now, as I understand it, a poll has been demanded. Is that so?
Mrs Vickers: Yes.
Mr Page: There is no advantage in it. You will not win.

This was turning out to be the most exciting, the only exciting, Board meeting since the early 1880s.

A Mr Phillips suggested a compromise of 500 guineas, agreeing to a certain extent with Mrs Vickers that the Board's remuneration was already high when compared with other companies.

Ernest Page was not having this and pointed out that the Managing Director's salary came out of the Directors' fees. Mr Phillips' suggestion of a compromise was not seconded and Ernest Page took control — this opposition was outrageous!

> Is that seconded? (There was no response.) If that is not seconded, Mr Weldon's motion is now put to the meeting; and it is my business as Chairman to order the poll either at once or after an interval or adjournment or otherwise. I order the poll now.
>
> Mr Tompkinson: May we know who it is suggests that a poll should be taken.
>
> Mrs Vickers: I do.
>
> Mr Page: Then I order the poll to be taken at once.

But others intervened to try to dissuade Mrs Vickers from forcing a vote. Mrs Vickers however stuck to her guns pointing out that the Directors' fees in 1905 only amounted to £1,500.

> Mr Page: It is not worth arguing with Mrs Vickers. She is entitled to a poll.

In the poll, a Mrs Tebbs, Mrs Vickers and Mrs Sinclair (three women!) voted against with 5,960 shares. The remaining shareholders, excluding the directors, voted for the resolution with 8,003 shares. It was not overwhelming but Ernest Page was to have the last word. He said that he had forgotten to mention that he had it under covenant that the property sold would never be used in such a way as to compete with the Grand.

1926 saw the first substantial advance in receipts and profits for some years (in spite — perhaps because — of the General Strike) and an increased dividend was paid on the increased capital. 1927 saw a further increase in spite of the appalling summer and 1928 a slight decrease in receipts and the 1920s drew to a close with a further slight decrease before the cold economic winds of the 1930s set in.

FARM DEVELOPMENTS

Apart from financial developments the 1920s was a period of great development in the Grand Hotel, primarily in the music sphere, but there was progress on other fronts too. You will remember that in 1920 the farm at Willingdon was still in its early days. By 1921 Ernest Page was able to tell the shareholders that out of eggs, pigs, vegetables and fruit a profit of £917 was made, representing a 27.75% return on capital and this in a year when the potato yield was lower than expected and when 1,000 plum trees did not produce a single plum and there were hardly any pears. Nevertheless 51 tons of potatoes were raised which supplied the hotel for eight to ten months. Cabbages, cauliflowers, beans and broccoli yielded £541, apples £346,

> and the people staying at the Hotel have been living on apples ever since — apple dumplings, apple fritters, roasted apples, apple tarts and so on — and they like them.

From the chickens came nearly 30,000 eggs. There were now pigs although these were the subject of a minor disaster and Ernest Page gave his sense of humour full vent in talking of it to the shareholders,

> We had a hideous brute of a sow, an enormous, ungainly beast, and this creature presented us with, I think it was, twelve little pigs, mostly healthy and funny little animals, and the old lady seemed pleased with them. But the pleasure did not last long, because she used them as a mattress, with the result that every one without exception was killed. I do not know what became of them; I can only imagine that they were served up to the Hotel visitors by our most valued chef, Murray, in the form of pancakes.

The company also made good use of the gardens at the Rosemount, one of the properties bought with the Sussex Club, and grew many flowers and a great deal of fruit there. The hotel had an abundance of flowers and the gardener won prizes and cups for his flowers, in particular a challenge cup for the finest chrysanthemums.

IMPROVEMENTS TO THE HOTEL

Improvements were continually made to the hotel including the purchase of a smart new omnibus in 1924 for picking up guests from the station. On the motor side also the serious deficiency of a small garage was rectified. More and more people were using cars and the existing garage would only accommodate 20. As a result people were having to leave their cars some distance away and the management felt that some were so annoyed by this they went to other resorts or hotels. They were therefore glad to buy a large garage in Silverdale Road, albeit at a cost of £8,000.

Inside the hotel it was the decade of the bathroom. It was no longer good enough to have communal bathrooms and maids bringing hot water to the rooms. Guests now demanded private bathrooms (perhaps it was those years in the army and the trenches with no baths at all). Thus each year bathrooms were added although it was not envisaged that every room should have a bathroom. In 1926 Ernest Page told shareholders,

> It is impossible for us to give, as might be done in the case of an absolutely new hotel, a bathroom to every bedroom; that is quite impossible.

But if each room could not have a bathroom then it could have running water and gradually in the middle 1920s each room was given this facility.

LIFE IN THE HOTEL———————————————————

Jack Richardson, who started in the hotel in 1928 and worked his way up through commis waiter to silver service waiter to head floor waiter and finally to restaurant manager, recalls that the man who ruled the roost in the 1920s was the fearsome Mr Gabb. Tall, waistcoated with a watch-chain, Gabb had a squint and he governed by respect and a touch of fear. Every waiter, including the commis waiters, had to say goodnight to Mr Gabb before they went off duty. Also every night a commis waiter and a page boy had to take his newspapers and magazines and a parcel to his house in Carew Road to await his arrival. Jack Richardson tells the story with a smile but also with a wary glance at the skies of how one night it was his turn to take the parcel. He could not open the gate into the garden and threw the parcel over the wall. The next day he was summoned by Gabb,

> Boy, I want you. Do you know what was in that parcel?
> No, sir.
> Eggs.

Gabb also made the commis waiters and page boys go to church every Sunday.

THE FAMOUS WERE STILL COMING———————————

The famous and wealthy were still coming to the hotel. Jack Richardson remembers Queen Marie of Yugoslavia and her son who became King Peter, also Sir John Ellerman, the shipping magnate and Lord and Lady Southwood, the owners of Odhams Press, the *Daily Herald* and *Illustrated London News*.

Two heroes of the day, Jim Mollison MBE and his wife Amy Johnson CBE, also stayed at the Grand. Both broke record after record in the world of aviation. Jim Mollison flew from England to Australia in July/August 1931 in 8 days, 19 hours, 28 minutes. The following year he established the record England to the Cape by West Coast of Africa route taking 4 days, 17 hours, 5 minutes. In the same year he also accomplished the first Westward solo Atlantic flight and in 1933 the first flight from England to South America. In 1934 he established the England—India record and in 1936 he flew from New York across Newfoundland to London establishing a coast to coast record of 9 hours 20 minutes. He was twice awarded the Gold Medal of the City of New York and also given the Freedom of Atlantic City.

His wife, Amy Johnson, also won great fame for her exploits. In 1930 she was the first woman to fly alone from London to Australia. In 1931 she flew to Japan and back setting a record both ways and the following year she flew to Cape Town and back again setting a record both ways. All this excitement in the family proved too much and the two were divorced later in the 1930s.

A star from a different world also came to the Grand, Paul Robeson. Robeson, the American negro singer, did perhaps more than anyone else to develop negro folk music. In 1928 he came to London and sang 'Ol' Man River' in *Show Boat* at Drury Lane and he also played the title role in *Othello* at the Savoy Theatre in 1930.

Steve Donoghue, the famous jockey, also came to the Grand to recover from breaking his legs in a fall and Jack Richardson can remember him betting Gilligan, the county cricketer, that he would not make a 100 before lunch the next day at the Saffrons. In the event he made it by 12 o'clock.

THE GRAND HOTEL ORCHESTRA————————————

To the visitors to the Grand Hotel the music of Van Lier and that of his successor, Arthur Beckwith, had been one of the great attractions of the hotel but it was Albert Sandler and the BBC broadcasts that gave the hotel and its music a whole new dimension.

The first outside broadcast by the BBC was at a hotel in Bournemouth. Sam Eeley, the manager of the Grand, heard it and immediately contacted the BBC. He told them of the wonderful acoustics of the lounge in his hotel and of the quality of his orchestra. They listened to him, tried his lounge and his orchestra and music was transmitted from the Grand Hotel, Eastbourne every Sunday night from 1924 until 1939.

THOSE FAMOUS ACOUSTICS————————————

Quite why the acoustics were so good in the lounge of the Grand no-one knows. The lounge had after all been built fifty years earlier and with its embellished balconies and fluted pillars and columns it had many irregularities of shape and design. Gerald Cock, the Director of Outside Broadcasts for the BBC in the 1920s and 1930s, maintained that the lounge had as fine acoustic properties for a small orchestra and singers as were to be found anywhere. He attributed them to the shape and proportion and the materials used fortuitous though these may have been. The columns were supposed to have been built of lime, cow hair, dung and chalk. Sam Eeley felt that the shape and the irregularity of design broke any echo.

ALBERT SANDLER————————————

Whatever the acoustics the music would not have flourished and the BBC programme would not have achieved popularity

Albert Sandler — the man with the "singing violin".

without the musicians. Foremost among them was Albert Sandler. The *Radio Times* in an article in July 1939 said this,

> When Albert Sandler at the youthful age of nineteen made his radio debut as leader on August 28, 1924, and introduced the orchestra to listeners, he won fame in a night for himself and for the Grand.

Ernest Page spoke of Albert to the shareholders,

> The new Chef d'Orchestre, Mr Sandler, is a Pole, a young man it is true, but a very splendid player of the violin. So good is he that we were asked to allow our band to be broadcast, which has been done on several occasions, and Mr Eeley and Mr Sandler have been almost snowed under with letters of congratulation from people in various parts of the country. some coming from Germany, some from the north of Scotland and some from various parts of France and this country. I hope that some of you will listen in, although, of course, I would much rather that you listened in the lounge of the Grand Hotel, because it would be more profitable than if you merely put those machines in your ears.

(I am sorry to bring Mr Page in yet again but his turn of phrase is quite remarkable.)

Ernest Page referred again in 1926 to the national and even international audience that Sandler had now acquired. He had met a man who had come specially to Eastbourne and to the Grand Hotel to hear Sandler. The reason he had come was because he had been listening-in in Burma, yes Burma, and he had heard,

> I am now taking you over to the Grand Hotel, Eastbourne, to hear the concert which will be broadcast there.

SANDLER'S MUSIC

What type of music did Sandler and his orchestra play?

A programme of Sunday, December 26, 1926, shows that the

Broadcast Programme

BY

ALBERT SANDLER

AND THE

Grand Hotel Orchestra

Sunday, December 26th, 1926,

Broadcast - - 9.15 to 10.45.

GRAND HOTEL : : : EASTBOURNE

An Albert Sandler programme.

evening performance was to be broadcast by the British Broadcasting Company through London and Daventry. The programme was,

Excerpts from 'La Bohème'	... Puccini
'L'Extase'	... Thome
Song 'Lasoia ohio pianga' (Rinaldo)	... Handel

Miss Edith Furmedge

Violin Solos —	
a. 'Prelude and Allegro'	... Pugnani Kreisler
b. 'Ave Maria'	... Schubert Wilhelmj

Albert Sandler

Piano Solo 'Fantasie in F Minor'	... Chopin

J.A. Byfield

Songs —
    a. 'O Lovely Night'   . . . Landon Ronald
    b. 'Abide with me'   . . . Liddle
                    (By Request)
                Miss Edith Furmedge

    Grand Fantaisie 'Pagliacci'   . . . Leoncavallo
                God Save the King
        During Solos Waiters will not be in attendance

The afternoon performance had included,

	Fletcher's	'Spirit of Pageantry'
	Wallace's overture	'Maritana'
	Rachmaninoff's	'Prelude' (in fact played as a solo by Jack Byfield)
	Lehar's	'The Merry Widow'
and	Ranzato's	'Passion'

The programme also displayed a photograph of the young handsome Albert Sandler with his dark wavy hair and advertised the fact that he recorded exclusively for Vocalion new electrical process records. A 12-inch record with Kreisler's arrangement of 'Londonderry Air' was on one side and Paul Rubens' 'Violin Song' on the other. The cost was 4s 6d (22.5p — perhaps £4.50 today).

Other records offered included,

Moszkowski's	'Serenata Op.15, No.1'
Paul Rubens'	'I Love the Moon'
Logan's	'Pale Moon' (An Indian Love Song)
Sanderson's	'Until'
Saint-Saëns'	'Le Cygne'
Kreisler's	'Tambourine Chinois'

Albert Sandler stayed at the Grand Hotel until 1928 and when he left he was interviewed by the *Eastbourne Gazette*. He was fulsome in his praise of both the Hotel and Eastbourne,

My first impression and my last is that it is a beautiful town; I shall always love it. To those in search of as nearly an ideal town as can be found in England, I recommend Eastbourne. Eastbourne is charming, the Grand Hotel is a luxury, the people are the most gracious and sympathetic I have ever met.

Asked why he was leaving he said it was to pursue his career to its best advantage.

He recalled how Princess Beatrice had visited the hotel and listened to his music. She had sent her gentleman-in-waiting to summon him to appear before her and had thanked him for his solo and asked him,

Would you like to play before the King and Queen?

Sandler had of course said yes and Princess Beatrice said she would have to see what could be arranged. (In fact if Sandler had stayed at the Grand he would have played to the future King Edward VIII and the future King George VI and Elizabeth his wife as they all visited the hotel at the end of the 1920s.)

Edward P

30-VI-31

Albert

Elizabeth

October 29th 1929

Oct: 29: 1929

The Prince of Wales, the future King Edward VIII, enjoying a quiet moment. (Photograph by courtesy of the BBC Hulton Picture Library.)

The Duke and Duchess of York (the future King George VI and Queen Elizabeth) visiting Eastbourne on 29 October 1929. More than 50,000 flags were distributed. (Photograph by courtesy of the BBC Hulton Picture Library.)

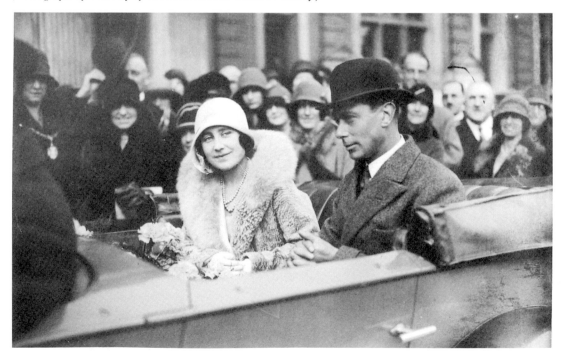

THE "SINGING" VIOLIN ————————————

People said that Sandler had a violin that sang. He appeared at concerts all over the country and to packed houses at the Queen's Hall. In Birmingham where he appeared twice a night for six nights the audience would scarcely allow him to leave the platform and insisted on a speech with every performance.

The reporter talked of his being a "master" of melody and his feature of treating light music in a classic style — "if classic stands for what is pure, elegant and refined, as distinct from the commonplace." He talked of his 'Down in the Forest', 'Wait' and 'Hush-a-bye Island' and his 'La Bohème', 'La Tosca' and 'Ave Maria'.

Albert Sandler with Jack Byfield and Reginald Kilbey.

Sandler left to play at the Park Lane Hotel in London and to continue his broadcasts. His fame was such that he appeared on one of the cigarette cards that were used to promote cigarettes between the wars. He was number twelve in a series of 50 Radio Celebrities. He died tragically young at the age of 42 in 1948. His life generally was not one of great happiness. Jewish from the East End of London, his mother wanted him to marry a nice Jewish girl called Edith. Instead he married at 18 a French girl called Raymonde who thanked him by leaving him for Johnson, the white haired partner of the famous black comedian pair, Layton and Johnson. He then married a Doreen who also left him and finally his third wife outlived him. None of them looked after him properly.

Tom Jones, who replaced him as leader of the orchestra at the Grand, recalls that Albert was a brilliant musician and a lovely man but perhaps a little naive. He remembers one or two funny incidents involving Albert. On one occasion Albert was talking to some "very rich and posh people" in the lounge at the Grand and he was telling them about his wife, Raymonde,

My wife is very clean. She washes herself under her arms.

On another occasion he and the piano player, Jack Byfield were having a heated discussion. Finally Jack said,

Be quiet, Albert, you argue like Aristotle.

To which Albert replied,

'Arry who? Was he a fiddle player?

But naive or not, Tom Jones acknowledges that it was Albert who put the music at the Grand on the map. According to Tom, Albert loved playing to the rich ladies. Tom himself, who succeeded him, preferred more classical music and after his six years at the Grand that is what he went back to.

TOM JONES

Tom Jones came from a totally different background from Albert Sandler. His father, James Jones, was a violinist, and the parents of his wife Marjorie had been a harpist and double bass player in the private orchestra of the Duke of Devonshire. Tom himself had been in the London Philharmonic under Thomas, later Sir Thomas Beecham whose assistant had been Malcolm, later Sir Malcolm, Sargent. Tom remembers Sargent with little affection. He recalls that one year they were forced to play over Christmas and received no overtime pay. When they complained Sargent said,

> The people who run this orchestra have their money tied up in shares. They can't sell them to pay you.

Tom Jones — the violinist with a sense of humour.

Nevertheless the musicians sued the orchestra and won though as Tom laughingly points out it did not do them any good as they all got the sack.

Tom comes from Birmingham and still calls his wife "Kidder". He and Marjorie certainly had some music in them. Their elder son, Michael was with Karajan in the Philharmonia Symphony Orchestra of London and then with the Amici Quartet. Their younger son Martin is Chairman of the Philharmonia and his daughter Karen won the wind section of the Young Musician of the Year competition in 1984 on the flute. His younger daughter Deborah won a scholarship as a singer to the Guildhall.

Tom recalls from his days at the Grand that Sir Thomas Beecham, Sir Hamilton Harty and Sir Landon Ronald came to hear them play. Sir Landon used to shake his fist at Tom because he would play one of his early, rather poor, compositions. Tom had, and still has, a great sense of humour. He can also remember the famous Fritz Kreisler and Jan Kubelik coming to the hotel. Kubelik would stride through the hotel lounge followed by a negro servant carrying his violin case. Unrelated to his musical performances Tom also tells of the story of Police Constable Roby.

Tom had met the dimwitted PC Roby when he had witnessed some car thieves pinch a car and had to suggest to Roby it might be best to chase them in a car. Sometime later, following a series of thefts of silver and pewter from the hotel Bill, the night porter, waited in the shadows of the lounge and sure enough an intruder came in and stole some more silver. Guess who was assigned to the case — PC Roby? No. In fact the dimwitted PC Roby was the thief and it turned out that his house was full of stolen silver.

CHAPTER FIVE

THE HUNGRY THIRTIES

MASS UNEMPLOYMENT ——————————————

In the late 1980s there is an unemployment level of over three million in the United Kingdom and while this is shocking it does not represent the same misery and deprivation that the three million unemployed of 1933 represented. At that stage three million was over 20% of the insured population, as opposed to 12% today, and the relief available was pitiably small. In the early 1930s an unemployed man whose insurance payments were in order and up-to-date could claim as of right benefit of 15s (75p but perhaps £15 today) for fifteen weeks. He could also claim a further small amount for dependants. After that, if he had still not found work but could show that he was genuinely looking for it and could also show that previously his insurance contributions had been paid regularly, he would go on to Transitional Benefit — i.e. "the dole". Men not covered by insurance contributions could apply for outdoor relief from the Public Assistance Committee of the local authorities. Incredibly because of the financial crisis of 1931 Transitional

95

Benefit levels were cut by 10% and were to be paid for only 26 weeks. These were renamed Transitional Payments and were to be paid by the Public Assistance Committees and only then after a stringent Means Test. The system was degrading and spiteful. The country suffered for it through the following forty years because of the resentments it caused.

As the working classes suffered, many in the middle classes suffered too. When factories closed the clerical staff and managers lost their jobs too, shareholders lost their investment and directors their fees. The early 1930s was not a happy time and we shall see that the Grand Hotel which had survived the Kaiser's War unscathed and had indeed boomed through it, was badly affected by the world protectionist war of the 1930s.

It was not, of course, all gloom and doom. There was growth in the economy in the second half of the decade. Indeed in housing and construction there was a mini-boom and much of the country's housing stock was built then. As Marwick points out in his book, *Britain in our Century* J.B. Priestley was able to find a diversified country in his book *English Journey* written in 1933,

There was, first, Old England, the country of cathedrals and minsters and manor houses and inns, of Parson and Squire; guidebook and quaint highways and byways England . . .

Then there is nineteenth century England, the industrial England of coal, iron, steel, cotton, wool, railways; of thousands of rows of little houses all alike, sham Gothic churches, square-faced chapels, Town Halls, Mechanics Institutes, mill foundries, warehouses, refined watering places . . .

Literary and Philosophical Societies, back to back houses, detached villas with monkey trees, Grill Rooms, railway stations, slag-heaps and tips, dock roads, Refreshment Rooms, doss-houses, Unionist or Liberal Clubs, cindery waste grounds, mill chimneys, slums, fried-fish shops, public houses with red blinds, bethels in corrugated iron, good class drapers' and confectioners' shops, a cynically devastated countryside, sooty dismal little towns, and still sootier grim fortress-like cities . . .

The third England was the new post-war England, belonging far more to the age itself than to this particular island. America, I suppose, was its real birth-place. This is the England of arterial and by-pass roads, of filling stations and factories that look like exhibition buildings (e.g. the Hoover factory at Perivale), of giant cinemas and dance-halls and cafes, bungalows with tiny garages, cocktail bars, Woolworths, motor-coaches, wireless, typing, factory girls looking like actresses, greyhound racing and dirt tracks, swimming pools and everything given away for cigarette coupons.

THE GRAND HOTEL — STILL A HAVEN OF LUXURY

How was the Grand Hotel coping with this difficult world? It did not change. It still offered the very best. Indeed an excellent and expensive brochure produced at the beginning of the 1930s waxed lyrically about the hotel,

> To live in surroundings in which Royalty has been entertained and yet retain the friendly comfort of your own home, to enjoy the calm of a beautifully appointed country house together with the endless conveniences of the modern hotel — here is an experience rare enough to merit description.

The brochure first described the beauties of West Sussex with Eastbourne as its Queen. It claimed that the town had occupied first, second and third places successively for the sunniest town in the British Isles and also claimed a higher average temperature than Bournemouth and rainfall far lower than Torquay (an early example of knocking copy!). It spoke of the hotel's 250 rooms that could accommodate 350 guests and of the large, spacious public rooms and also of the

> Winter Garden at the main entrance, with its white woodwork and curved glass roof.

The brochure emphasised that almost every member of the staff was British — a contrast with pre-war days when many had been German and Austrian and when Van Lier had changed his name to Von Leer to appear to be German.

THE FAMOUS LOUNGE HALL

Here is how the brochure described the famous Lounge Hall,

Through the swing doors which, on each side keep this room free from outside noise, you enter the Lounge part of which is the celebrated Lounge Hall. Here are given those delightful concerts, so familiar to radio listeners everywhere, 'relayed from the Grand Hotel, Eastbourne'. This hall has acoustics that are little short of amazing. It is regarded by broadcasting experts as the most perfect hall for radio transmission in the world.

The orchestra — "relayed from the Grand Hotel".

Designed in Georgian style, with a touch of colour, this is one of the pleasantest parts of the Hotel, as well as one of the most notable. It is forty feet high and has balconies on the first and second floors. The Lounge, the Lounge Hall and the adjoining Drawing Room are decorated in cream and green, giving the freshness of Spring the whole year through.

The Grand Hotel chefs — let's hope the food was less fearsome.

The brochure of course mentioned the fruit, flowers and vegetables coming from the hotel's own farm and nursery and described the dining room as one hundred and ten feet long and thirty five feet wide with a seating capacity of 350. (It did not mention the "separate tables" — this was the norm by now.) It noted the twenty amber electric bowls and the fact that diners looked directly on to the sunlit lawns through eight full length windows.

The cellars, forty feet below, also received high praise, with the temperature never varying more than two degrees, winter or summer. It talked of thousands of pounds worth of fine Cliquot, Chambertin, Chateau Yquem and ports dating back to 1887, a thirty five year old sherry and a seventy year old brandy.

The bedrooms themselves now all had hot and cold running water, the hot water being both softened and, "in this Hotel, indisputably hot!" Every bedroom also had a telephone and the guests could choose between two types of fire, coal or electric. Each bed had a deep box-spring mattress and a separate spring mattress on top.

There were still plenty of nurses and nannies and the brochure made it clear that they were also well catered for and also that there was a nursery for the children. There was also a gentlemen's and ladies' hairdressing salon and there were still the electric and medical baths with the services of a masseur and chiropodist. In the main body of the hotel there were now three electric lifts — the old hydraulic one with its difficult ropes had gone.

Outside, the brochure boasted of its garage facilities,

> Now, since modern man is helpless without his car and a good motorist watches it as, a hundred years ago, he would have watched the tending of his horse, let us go out to the garages. Here are sixty self-contained lock-ups, with chauffeurs' quarters near by and an experienced mechanic in charge, who can not only give every service, but supply any of the dozen and one necessities of the road. The garages are at the corner of Compton Street and Jevington Gardens. On the west side of the Hotel is Silverdale Road, in which there is also an entrance.

For outside activities the brochure talked of tennis, badminton, squash rackets, riding, boating, swimming, the East Sussex Fox-hounds, bowls, crocquet, fishing and golf with the three courses at Royal Eastbourne, Eastbourne Downs and Willingdon. For

An aerial view of the hotel in the 1930s. The conservatory and tennis court are still there, as is the cabbies' stand.

entertainment there was the theatre, the Winter Garden Concerts, Thés Dansants and Carnivals. In the nearby Devonshire Park there were the famous lawn tennis courts where the South of England Lawn Tennis Tournament took place every September. Davis Cup and other international matches were also played here. Finally, first class cricket was played at the Saffrons ground.

The brochure then took us back inside to the Grand Hotel in the evening where there was an American Bar in the Smoking Room with its deep leather armchairs and array of magazines. Next to the Smoking Room was the Billiards Room. Both rooms had large open fires. After dinner of course there would be coffee in the lounge listening to the hotel orchestra. If it were a Saturday there would be a dance in the magnificent Ballroom with high curved ceiling of intricate design, its deep windows, and panelled walls divided by wide pillars. Hanging from the ceiling would be five giant illuminated baskets of flowers sending many-coloured gleams of light over the dancers. This Ballroom with its special spring floor would hold 600 people.

A dance in the ballroom with its special sprung floor.

The brochure pointed out that all this luxury still only cost a moderate price and included a tariff. Judge for yourself. You should perhaps multiply the prices by 20 to allow for inflation to 2000,

Single bedroom	from 8/6 (42.5p or perhaps	£8.50)
Double bedroom	from 17/6 (87.5p '' ''	£17.50)
Bedroom with private bathroom	from 22/6 (£1.12½p '' ''	£22.50)
Private Sitting Room	from 15/- (75p '' ''	£15.00)
Private Sitting Room with bedroom	from 35/- (£1.75p '' ''	£35.00)
Private Sitting Room with bedroom & bathroom	from 42/- (£2.10p '' ''	£42.00)
Self-contained suites	from 52/6 (£2.62½ '' ''	£52.50)

Breakfasts

Table d'hote from 8.30 to 10.30	4/- (20p or perhaps	£4.00)
Plain breakfast - Boiled eggs, toast, preserves	3/- (15p ″ ″	£3.00)
Plain breakfast - Tea, coffee, cocoa or chocolate with bread and butter	2/6 (12.5p ″ ″	£2.50)

Luncheons

Table d'hote from 1 to 2.30	5/- (25p ″ ″	£5.00)
Table d'hote to non-Residents	5/6 (27.5p ″ ″	£5.50)

Teas

Cup of tea or coffee	9d (4p ″ ″	75p)
Cup of tea with bread and butter, cake etc.	1/6 (7.5p ″ ″	£1.50)
Cup of tea with bread and butter, cake etc. to non-Residents on Sunday	2/6 (12.5p) ″ ″	£2.50)

Dinners

Table d'hote from 7 to 8.30	7/6 (37.5p ″ . ″	£7.50)

Children (under ten years of age)

Board in Nursery	per day 8/6 (42.5p ″ ″	£8.50
Board in Private or Coffee Room	per day 12/6 (62.5p ″ ″	£12.50)

Visitors' Servants

Bedroom and Board in Steward's Room	per day 12/6 (62.5p ″ ″	£12.50)
Bedroom and Board in Steward's Room (in Season)	per day 15/- (75p ″ ″	£15.00)

Fires

Sitting or bedroom fire	per day 4/- (20p ″ ″	£4.00)
Sitting or bedroom fire per half day	3/- (15p ″ ″	£3.00)
Bedroom evening fire	2/- (10p ″ ″	£2.00)

There were also inclusive terms for stays of more than three days and special terms for long visits. A large dining room on the ground floor was specially reserved for children and nurses. Nurses in uniform were not allowed in any of the public rooms and dogs, in uniform or not, were definitely not allowed in any of the public rooms. Visitors were also requested not to allow them to run about the Corridors and Staircases (the dogs not the nurses). In no case were large dogs allowed in the hotel but provision could be made for them outside. The charge for dogs was 2/6 (12.5p or perhaps £2.50). There was a note on the tariff that visitors bringing their own spirits or wine would be charged corkage.

Mrs Eeley — mother to guests and staff alike.

Thus the Grand Hotel was ready to offer the utmost luxury and service at "reasonable prices". It had recently entertained the Prince of Wales, the Duke and Duchess of York (the future King George VI and Queen Elizabeth), the Emperor and Empress of Japan, the King and Queen of the Hellenes and the Emir of Transjordania. Outside, Wall Street crashed, banks in Europe closed their doors, Hitler rose to power, and unemployment soared. What was the result?

EVEN THE GRAND HOTEL SUFFERS ——————

The immediate result was that business fell away quite sharply. Receipts of £155,000 in 1928 declined to £149,000 in 1929, to £129,000 in 1930, and to £112,000 in 1931. The Directors cut their fees by 25% and Cecil Page, who had replaced his father, Ernest as Chairman, felt the coming year would be equally difficult. Annual dinners were being cancelled and people were coming for shorter visits and asking for lower terms. The

Sam Eeley — the calm and long-serving manager. He is seated on the right, wearing a carnation. Others in the main group from left to right — Edward Watt's father, Mrs Sam Eeley, Violet Eeley, Edward Watt and Edward Watt's mother. The photograph was taken in the dining room at the Grand on the occasion of the Staff Sports Club prize presentation coupled with Violet Eeley's 21st and engagement party.

interim dividend was cut and Cecil Page could see no prospect of its being re-instated in the near future. In 1932 business declined further. Receipts were down to £98,000 and the net profit fell £3,600 to £13,638. The drop was not fully accounted for by a drop in the number of visitors, which fell only 4.5% but by lower expenditure by those who came. Cecil Page noted that the visits by parents at half-term at the many Eastbourne schools had shown a marked decline. He was not sure whether this was because the parents no longer visited the children or because they only visited them for the day.

Income declined yet again in 1933 to £96,696 but the company managed to push profits up by £874 to £14,512. This was attributed to the phenomenal summer (we usually have one every fifteen years), low commodity prices and strenuous efforts to curtail expenditure. By now some of the shareholders were becoming restless and the annual general meeting, held each year at the Langham Hotel, Portland Place, London, heard an outburst of criticism to rival that of Mrs Vickers in 1925. This time, however, it attempted to be a little more constructive. A Mr Eggar praised the staff, criticised the half per cent increase on the dividend as inadequate and went on to say,

I do think there are some things that are not very good about the Hotel. Let me take, first of all, the entrances. Neither the entrance in Compton Street nor the front of the hotel are at all good. Visitors coming into the reception room have to go through the lounge, often when music is in progress, and that is rather disturbing. Then the lounge in the middle of a hot sunny day; the whole of it has to be lit with electric light. Now, people go down to the sea for sun, light and air and I do not think the lounge is quite what it should be. As for the winter garden, I think it is a very poor winter garden and not worth advertising ... What I would suggest is this, that take your carriage drive for instance with an entrance from the promenade. It is a very poor entrance. I would make that entrance from Jevington Gardens. It might involve scrapping something that is no good. Then the car park is very poor. There is not room for many cars, and if you have to turn round on a busy day it is an awful business. I suggest you can make a sunken car park in the south-west corner of the grounds. Then I should suggest you can get rid of a lot of shrubs and some part of the wall, so as to make the outlook brighter for people who are in the lounge. Then, instead of the present reception room, I would suggest that you should make a new entrance to the hotel where rooms 11, 12 and 13 are present. [There is no room No. 13 these days; many people will not stay in room No. 13!] That is just on the west of the dining room, and then scrap the present winter garden and build out where the present winter garden is, a fine lounge, and you could have bedrooms on top, in fact a new building. I know it would cost a good deal, but you would get light, sun and air which is so much needed. I do think that the lounge, although it is magnificent in its way, is not a fit lounge, for a Hotel of the standing of the Grand, where you do want to see the sun, light and air which you ought to get.

This was all a great contrast to the superlatives we read earlier in the chapter in the hotel's brochure. Cecil Page agreed that the lounge was not as sunny as it might be but again drew everyone's attention to its acoustic qualities. He also defended the garden and the small parking area pointing out that if they were not careful they would have one large asphalt car park.

A Dr Colgate was also critical of the shrubs,

The shrubs curtail the space and in every way are deleterious especially when we have a wall in front which stands 5ft. 6ins. high, and above that there is at least another 2ft. which very often amounts to 5ft., for the screen which shuts out the light and shuts in the view.

Dr Colgate also criticised the back entrance,

You arrive there and it is called a reception place, but it is a narrow entrance with, on one side, a chemist's shop, which of course is not the most delightful thing to see, and on the other side there is a so-called Turkish Bath. Then there is no lift to take the invalids up to the Hotel; they have to walk up or go up in a luggage lift.

Dr Colgate then got quite angry with the directors, haranguing them for sitting with the sun behind them so that he could not see their faces. This raised a smile which made him even more angry.

Cecil Page nevertheless answered the criticisms. He agreed that the Compton Street entrance was not entirely satisfactory but any alteration would be prohibitively expensive (as we shall see no alterations were ever made and eventually it was no longer used as a main entrance after the mid 1950s). The garden was sunk and at least afforded some protection from the wind. The hotel could not be raised to give the ground floor a view of the sea,

> You have only to go up to the first-floor rooms and there you have a complete view of the sea.

The wall in the garden could be removed but Mr Page was sure no one would want the noise and smell of the motor cars.

The Board were in a cleft stick. Competition was severe and shareholders wanted their hotel to be clearly pre-eminent. But because competition was so severe the revenue was not being earned that would allow expensive modifications.

HOTEL IMPROVEMENTS IN THE 1930s

Nevertheless the hotel did continue a limited modernisation programme throughout the 1930s. The coal-fired boilers were converted to take fuel oil and by 1932 this work had been completed bringing a saving in costs and a cleaner atmosphere.

The ridiculous thing was that in the following year the Chancellor of the Exchequer imposed a tax on heavy oils of a penny a gallon to discourage the buying of foreign oil and encourage the purchase of British coal. This wiped out any savings the Grand might have made converting to oil and the hotel was forced to re-convert three of its boilers to coal.

Many electric fires were also purchased as a number of guests preferred them to coal fires in their rooms. This necessitated a complete re-wiring of the hotel which was carried out in 1933. By 1934 the hotel had overhauled the central heating system which covered the public rooms and also installed it in the front rooms of the centre block of the hotel. In 1935, stung perhaps by the criticism received at the annual general meeting of 1933, the old Winter Gardens at the front entrance was replaced by a new sun lounge. The old glass and iron structure erected 33 years earlier was removed and Cecil Page noted that he had not heard any expressions of regret. In fact he had to admit that,

> The sun lounge is modern and up-to-date and although it occupies the same floor area as the old structure, the removal of the wood and glass screens has given us a much more spacious place with plenty of light and air, and it also has the advantage of making the hall very much lighter.

Mr Eggar and Dr Colgate were no doubt delighted but if so, they did not stand up and say so, perhaps confining themselves to a murmured "Hear, hear".

By 1937 every room in the hotel had its own centrally heated radiator. We can be sure that one person who will have appreciated this will have been the Emperor Haile Selassie who had been forced to flee Ethiopia when it was invaded and overrun by Mussolini in 1936. This, of course, was the famous test case for the League of Nations and the Emperor went to Switzerland to plead for help for his nation. All he got was some useless and ineffectual sanctions. The League, set up with such hope and idealism in 1919, had failed. Mussolini and, more importantly, Adolf Hitler, took due heed. Haile Selassie came to England. At the request of the British Government he came incognito. Nevertheless the streets of London were lined with cheering crowds, shouting "Haile Selassie".

While negotiations continued on his behalf the Emperor wanted quiet luxury. Where else but the Grand Hotel? The

Haile Selassie — everyone stood up and clapped. (Photograph by courtesy of the BBC Hulton Picture Library.)

Emperor came for a few days before moving to Fairfield, a house in Bath where he remained until his return to Ethiopia in 1940. Apparently, when he entered the restaurant at the hotel everyone stood up and clapped him.

The central heating had taken three years to complete and had cost £6,000 (perhaps £120,000 today). In 1938 nothing very radical was done but the dining room was recarpeted and cost £500 (perhaps £10,000 today) and 150 bedrooms were re-decorated and another 75 reupholstered. A further five private bathrooms were added bringing the total to 72 private bathrooms and 30 public ones. Someone suggested that the hotel could be brightened by an exterior wash. (This was one of the first things De Vere did in 1967 when they bought the Grand.) The Board went as far as obtaining estimates in 1938, discovered that the cost would be £2,000 to £3,000 or anything up to 25% of the hotel's net profit, and shelved the idea.

In 1934 both receipts and profits improved and Cecil Page was talking of restoring some of the cuts made in Directors' fees. (In fact, Page himself took no cut in fees until the Second World War came along. Nor indeed did any of the others. When the famous cut was made in 1930/1 the £750 lost was more than made up by Ernest Page no longer taking his £1,200.) Page also congratulated the Board on not cutting the staff's wages although such cuts did occur throughout the hotel industry. 1935 showed a further improvement and 1936 another increase. Receipts by then had climbed from £94,000 in 1933 to £119,000 in 1936, an increase of 25% and highly creditable. But it was still not the £150,000 plus earned in the early 1920s and from then until the outbreak of Hitler's War receipts declined. Cecil Page did point out the illogicality of some of the licensing laws in England,

> The licensing restrictions are anything but helpful and enough to drive people out of the country for their holidays; they are not even as good as in Scotland, where at least you can get a drink out of hours if you walk or drive to the next village. You can play golf, tennis, cricket or football on a Sunday in England, but you still cannot knock a ball about on a wet Sunday in licensed premised. I hope that some day we will get a little more logical. [It took some decades, Mr Page.]

In 1938 Cecil Page told the shareholders how lucky they were to receive a dividend of 7% and pointed out how hotel groups all over the country were reducing their dividends,

> De Vere Hotels, which includes the Royal Crescent, Brighton, and the Grand Pump Room, Bath — no dividend against 6 per cent; the Palace Hotel, Torquay — 2.5 per cent against 5 per cent; Queen Anne's Mansions — 9 per cent against 19 per cent; and Whitehall Court 2.5 per cent against seven and a half per cent.

In 1939, just before the Second World War, receipts dropped yet again to £95,714. It had been a difficult decade for income and profits. How did the hotel fare in other ways?

MEMORIES OF THE 1930s

It began with a visit for lunch by the Prince of Wales when he opened a new wing at the hospital. It continued with enjoyable visits for those who could still afford to come. Mrs Marjorie Wells was a telephonist at the hotel and remembers those days well,

> Fridays and Saturdays were great days for the staff, so busy and waiting to see who, and what well-known persons were arriving on the Grand Hotel's own big black bus which used to travel to the station to meet the London trains. Out would jump a porter and help folks up the few steps of the bus and then pile on the luggage.
>
> Amongst many guests were Evelyn Laye and her mother, the Salmon and Gluckstein family, the Kleenans.
>
> When the tennis tournament prior to Wimbledon was due there were Fred Perry and Bunny Austin. This was usually a hectic occasion as the Duke of Devonshire's statue come morning had a chamber pot on his head and toilet paper festooned around him.

Tom Jones, leader of the orchestra, remembers that the orchestra stopped playing because of all the noise the tennis stars were making. (And we thought that McEnroe and Connors were a modern phenomenon!) Back to Mrs Wells,

> In the evening the ballroom came into its glory where some of the most gorgeous gowns were on display. Jenkie as she was known was the dance hostess. Mrs Dreyfus or Minnie as she was called was usually sitting watching with Mr Charles Adams. Dr Bodkin Adams also came with partner [more about him later].
>
> Mr and Mrs S. Eeley were the managing directors and very much respected by the staff and visitors. Mrs Eeley was almost a mother to us young office staff — so kind but firm.

Everyone remembers the Eeleys with great affection. Mrs Finch, whose father Ernie Wilson worked as a cook in the hotel in the 1920s and 1930s for £3 10s a week, recalls that Sam Eeley was instrumental in helping them to move from a very damp house in Marine Parade to a much drier one in South Avenue.

Staff Children's Party — every child received a present.

The staff parties at Christmas are still talked about. The guests subscribed to them and indeed helped to serve at them. Every child of the staff received a present.

Mrs Violet Watt, Mr and Mrs Eeley's daughter, remembers that her mother would go round all the suites at 6 o'clock every evening to make sure all her guests were comfortable. Mrs Watt also remembers that on Sunday mornings after Church and while the maids cooked lunch Eastbourne society paraded itself on the Western Lawns in front of the Grand Hotel. That was the place to find yourself a wife or husband!

Incidentally Mrs Watt also remembers that her father discovered the great Albert Sandler playing in a Lyons Tea Shop in London. And talking of music, how was the orchestra faring in this difficult decade?

THE ORCHESTRA IN THE 1930s ——————————

The orchestra fared very well. Tóm Jones led it with great charm and skill until 1934 when Leslie Jeffries took his place. Jeffries was considered by some to be the best of all the violinist leaders of that type of orchestra.

Mrs "Jill" Byfield (her real name is Rose and for some reason people called her Girly. She did not like that and adopted the name Jill) remembers the 1930s when her husband, the famous pianist Jack Byfield played in the Grand Hotel orchestra. Apart from Jack on the piano and Tom or Leslie on the violin, there was Tom Hinkinson on the double bass, Louis Cramer on the cello and his brother, Fred Cramer on the mustel organ. (Michelle Jenkins, wife of Tom Jenkins about whom we shall hear soon, maintains that it was the mustel organ that gave the orchestra its lush sound. Without it the orchestra would have sounded rather thin.) The Cramers incidentally had come from Germany before the First World War and had been interned in a camp at Tunbridge Wells during the War. Jill Byfield can remember the lounge in pale green and gold with a plum coloured carpet the ladies in beautiful coloured gowns and the men in tails or at least dinner jackets. Those not in evening dress went to the balconies — from where no doubt they could see the BBC microphone hanging in the chandelier. Jill can also remember the head waiter, Mr Morse, otherwise known as Morsey, standing by the service door listening to the solos and not allowing any drinks to be served during these solos.

Mrs Ware, who was at the School of Domestic Economy in Silverdale Road opposite the hotel, used to come to dancing classes in the Ballroom run by the School's owner, Miss Randall. Of course they learned the Waltz and the Foxtrot, but perhaps surprisingly also the Tango and the Rhumba. Mrs Ware can remember that she and her fellow pupils would scuttle past Tom Jones while he was playing.

Western Lawns on Sunday morning — this was the place to find a wife or husband.

Tom Jones and his orchestra — from left to right, Louis Cramer, Jack Byfield (piano),
Harry Cousden, Tom Jones, Freddie Cramer (mustel organ), Tom Hinkinson.

The orchestra wore evening dress to play and the audience to listen, but most of the orchestra could not afford a car. John Stephens remembers that Walter Rolls, who played the double bass for a time would cycle down from Church Street and leave his bicycle on the pedal, and unlocked, on the pavement outside the Compton Street entrance. The performance over, he would cycle home again.

If Mrs Ware had not scuttled through the hall where the orchestra was playing she might have noticed those two famous tenors of the inter-war years, Richard Tauber and John MacCormack. The Austrian Tauber was already well known in German speaking countries when he took this country by storm in 1931 when he sang in Lehar's '*Das land des Lachelns*' at Drury Lane. MacCormack, an Irishman, was famous both here and in the USA for his renderings of Mozart, Handel, the Italian classics and German lieder. In 1928 he was made a papal count by Pope Pius XI and music lovers still enjoy LP re-issues of such favourites as Mozart's '*Il mio tesoro*' and Handel's '*O Sleep*'.

The orchestra's day off was Wednesday and on that day they indulged their hobbies whether they were golf, swimming or prawning. Louis Cramer, the cellist, loved prawning and would take Jack and Jill Byfield on his motor bicycle with sidecar leaving soon after dawn. Jack Byfield had studied from an early age with Dr Cambridge and Adolph Mann and he and Tom Jones had been at the Royal College of Music together where they studied with Sir Charles Stanford, Vaughan Williams and Gustav Holst. Two of Jack's most famous arrangements were 'Limelight' and 'David of the White Rock'. We shall meet Jack again in the story of the Grand in the 1950s.

TOM JENKINS

In 1938 the young and brilliant violinist Tom Jenkins, took over leadership of the orchestra from Leslie Jeffries. He was soon receiving copious fan mail and rave revues,

Mr Tom Jenkins is presenting attractive and excellently played programmes at the Grand Hotel, supported by instrumentalists of proved ability. On Sunday evening the bill of fare was on the popular side on the whole, but the items were presented with such musicianly clarity and sense of form that the lightest piece was made acceptable and enjoyable. A rich, full volume of tone was secured in the large orchestra pieces such as the "Tannhauser overture"; beautifully delicate effects were secured in the Elgar "Carissima" and the Saint-Saens Scherzo (a clever arrangement by Mr Sydney Ffoulkes, the pianist); Mr Jenkins's solos ("Caprice Viennoise" of Kreisler and Sarasate's "Zapateado", with the E flat Chopin Nocturne as an encore) were played with finish and skill.

Tom Jenkins — "you made at least one heart, if not many, very happy with such beautiful music."

A servant girl in London wrote,

I am only a maidservant but I am a musician at heart . . . you made at least one heart, if not many, very happy with such beautiful music.

Another listener wrote,

> Isn't "Dancing Daffodils" a lovely thing? So dainty and refreshing. And as you played it I pictured those lovely blooms nodding their heads in the glorious sunshine on a spring morning, far from the madding crowd.

The violin with which Tom Jenkins produced this lovely music was a Gagliano, an Italian violin about 140 years old. He had bought it from another well-known violinist, David McCallum, leader of the London Philharmonic Orchestra. When McCallum heard the broadcast from the Grand Hotel he sent a note to Tom,

> I did not think it could be the same fiddle. It sounded too good.

The orchestra that played with Tom at the Grand in 1938 and 1939 was,

Mr Sydney Ffoulkes	— piano
Mr Fred Cramer	— mustel organ
Mr Len Gold	— sub-leader
Mr Henry Cousden	— second violin
Mr Keith Cummings	— viola
Mr Louis Cramer	— cello
Mr Tom Hinkinson	— double-bass

Sydney Ffoulkes was well known as a composer as well as a pianist. Henry Cousden was the only member of the orchestra to have played in every broadcast from the Grand Hotel. Frederick Cramer had run concerts in France and his brother Louis was very proud of the fact that he had played the first note ever to be broadcast from the Grand Hotel — the famous opening of the *William Tell* overture. The Cramer brothers were also responsible for all the special arrangements used by the orchestra. Tom Hinkinson was originally the cellist in the Eastbourne Municipal Orchestra. Finally an occasional member of the orchestra Keith Cummings, a viola pupil of

Tom Jenkins with his orchestra — "The Grand Hotel lounge is easily the most perfect hall I have ever played in."

Lionel Tertis, was often heard on the air as a soloist or with various well-known small orchestras.

Tom himself confirmed what others had said of the acoustics of the Lounge Hall at the Grand,

> The Grand Hotel lounge is easily the most perfect hall I have ever played in. At my audition the quality and volume of sound completely amazed me. One can quite understand why huge sums of money have been spent in trying to copy such a hall. (The BBC apparently tried to reproduce the lounge on a set in London. It was not successful.)

Unfortunately, the next great war was approaching and the Grand enjoyed less than two years of Tom Jenkins as the leader of its orchestra. His distinguished career continued until he died of lung cancer in 1957, at the age of only 47. He had married Violet Harrop the pianist and after divorcing her married the beautiful star singer Dorothy Bond. Dorothy was tragically killed in a car crash at the age of 32 and Tom married Michelle Croft, a flautist in the orchestra at Scarborough. Michelle remembers that when they became engaged in 1953 congratulations were sent to the Grand Hotel even though Tom had not played there since 1940.

THE WAR APPROACHES

As war loomed again only twenty years after the previous blood-letting, Mrs Wells gives us her picture of life at the Grand Hotel — the smart hotel black bus picking up the guests from the station with the staff eager to see who is arriving; the little gold tables and the waltzes and foxtrots in the ballroom; Olive Grove singing for the BBC broadcasts; the girls from Clovelly Keppelston, the exclusive school, in their black hats and white coats; the boys from Eastbourne College walking from the foot of Beachy Head to the bandstand on Sunday mornings. The rhythm and tradition were all soon to end.

CHAPTER SIX

ANOTHER WAR

THE OVERALL EFFECT OF THE WAR

The Second World War was longer and more destructive than the First though losses among the fighting forces were much lower, half in fact at 300,000, because there were not the appalling set-piece battles that there had been between 1914 and 1918. The whole population was totally involved whether through air raids — 60,000 civilians were killed — or through hardship and rationing. 35,000 merchant seamen were lost in trying to bring vital supplies to the country. They were not always successful and rationing became severe, except perhaps by the standards of those besieged in Stalingrad. By the middle of 1941 the weekly ration of foods was a shilling's worth of meat (about half a lb) 1 oz of cheese, 4 oz of bacon or ham, 8 oz of sugar, 2 oz of tea, 8 oz of fats (including not more than 2 oz of butter) and 2 oz of jam or marmalade. The effect on society was profound and to see how this affected the Grand we must wait for an account of the aftermath of the war in the next chapter.

EASTBOURNE DURING THE WAR ——————————

You will remember that the Grand Hotel had taken out an insurance policy during the First World War against enemy action, first from the air, and then from the sea. It had scarcely been expected, no more than a remote possibility. This time it seemed that air raids would be a certainty and indeed the first air raid warning siren sounded within hours of the declaration of war. This proved a false alarm. The use of gas was also feared and most people carried respirators. At a wedding breakfast at the Grand on 3 September 1939 all the guests carried gas masks. For a time all the cinemas and other places of entertainment were closed until the Government realised the disastrous effect on morale of this regulation.

There was the phoney war period through the first winter. Jack Breach, who was Director of Publicity for Eastbourne Corporation in the post-war years, remembers that the 1939 Christmas was lively with plenty of visitors. For some reason

The SS Barnhill *on the beach — the staff and guests helped all through the night.*

Eastbourne was initially designated a safe area and London children were evacuated here. That was to change in the middle of 1940 when not only they but everyone else not doing an essential job was evacuated away from Eastbourne. The population declined to 8,000. Those who remained put cards on their front doors with the names of those living in the house. Thus in the event of an air raid everyone could be accounted for more easily. But on 20 March 1940 the reality was brought home to the people of Eastbourne when the SS *Barnhill* was bombed off Beachy Head and some of the crew were killed. The staff and some of the guests of the Grand worked all through the night to help the survivors. The ship eventually broke up and was beached whereupon crowds thronged the shore to salvage the tinned food. The Eastbourne sailing and fishing community responded to the call of the Government to help with the evacuation of British and French soldiers from Dunkirk in May 1940. Several vessels sailed across including the pleasure boats *Enchantress*, *Eastbourne Queen*, *Britannia*, *Grace Darling* and *Eastbourne Belle*, the fishing boat, *Commodore* and the lifeboat *Jane Holland*. The *Enchantress*, *Eastbourne Queen* and *Commodore* were all sunk but the others survived although the *Jane Holland* was badly damaged.

On 7 June 1940 the air raid siren was heard again for the first time since the false alarm of the previous September and on 23 June a train load of evacuees was sent to Wales. The King, George VI, visited the South Coast on 1 July and on 7 July Eastbourne received its first air raid when several bombs fell in the Whitley Road area. On that same day a ban on visitors to the town was imposed and shortly afterwards the Grand Hotel closed as indeed did the Queen's and the Cavendish. On 21 July 3,000 Eastbourne children were evacuated to Hertfordshire and Bedfordshire. On 16 August 1940 some Luftwaffe aeroplanes, being chased by RAF fighters, dropped bombs in the Hampden Park area and killed three corporation employees. This no doubt gave added impetus to a fund which was launched to raise £5,000 — the cost of a Spitfire — and the target was reached within ten days. On 13 September the town was heavily bombed and from then on air raids continued regularly into 1941. On Easter Friday 1941 a number of people tried to come to Eastbourne for a day by the sea but were turned back by the police. This was in stark contrast to Easter 1940 when the town had welcomed 30,000 visitors. On 19 April 1941 compulsory fire-watching for men between 18 and 60 was instituted and later that month War Weapons Week was opened by the Lord Chancellor, Viscount Simon, with a target of £250,000. This was reached within four days and the week's total was finally £502,243.

Evacuees at Eastbourne station — initially declared a Safe Area, it was soon clear Eastbourne was far from safe.

The Fire Station and Technical Institute after a direct hit — Eastbourne lost 174 people, killed in air raids.

Terminus Road after a raid — 671 high explosive and 3,625 incendiary bombs fell on the town.

Winston Churchill found time to visit the town. (Photograph by courtesy of the BBC Hulton Picture Library.)

On 13 May 1941 a realistic gas exercise was carried out in the main streets of Eastbourne using tear gas but in November 1941 came the first piece of good news — the ban on visitors was lifted. This brought a flood of bookings for Christmas for any hotel that was open or could be opened (as we shall see this did not include the Grand which had been requisitioned by the Government). Easter 1942 brought a visit from the Prime Minister, Winston Churchill. This was unexpected and there were few people at the station when he arrived. Word soon spread however and there were thousands to cheer him when he left.

On 4 May 1942 the town received its first air raid for eleven months. This was carried out by nine Luftwaffe bombers and amongst other damage the east wing of the Cavendish Hotel was demolished. Continuous, if spasmodic, raids continued through 1942 and into 1943, the last serious one coming on 4

June 1943. On 5 June 1942 the Duke of Kent visited the town and in December of that year a bus curfew at 9 pm was imposed. Fund raising was successful with over £500,000 being raised in both Wings for Victory Week in June 1943 and Salute the Soldier Week in June 1944. The aim of the Wings for Victory Week was to raise enough money — £500,000 — to buy 100 fighters. (A hundred fighters for the RAF today would cost £200 million.)

The Cavendish Hotel, once part of the same group as the Grand, received a direct hit.

1944 brought gradually better news from the fighting fronts but the South of England now had to suffer the terrors of the V1 and V2 flying bombs. The V1 you could at least hear and it was only when the whirring noise of its engine stopped that you knew it was about to fall. The V2 was altogether more horrific as it flew faster than sound and the first you knew about it was when it blew you to pieces.

AIR RAID STATISTICS ————————————————

Eastbourne suffered more air attacks than any other town in the South East region — 96. There were 1,346 alerts and 858 cuckoo warnings. There were 174 deaths, 443 serious injuries and 489 slight injuries. 671 high explosive bombs fell on the town and 3,625 incendiary bombs. 475 houses were destroyed, 1,000 were badly damaged and 10,000 slightly damaged. Mercifully the Grand Hotel was not hit though there were several near misses. The closest bomb was at the corner of Jevington Gardens which caused slight damage to the old store rooms. Perhaps the reason Eastbourne was raided so often was its pivotal position. On nearby Beachy Head the RAF set up a listening post for aircraft in distress. Beachy Head was also used as an assembly point for Douglas Bader's famous "Bus Company".

A map of where the bombs landed in Eastbourne. One or two got quite close to the Grand.

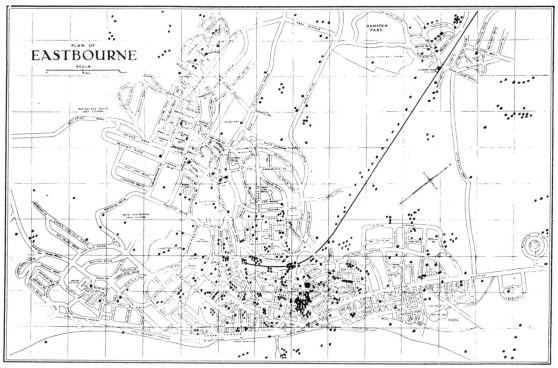

Beachy Head — a useful landmark for both the Germans and the British.
(Photograph by courtesy of Aerofilms Ltd.)

THE GRAND HOTEL DURING THE WAR

How did the Grand cope with all these trials and tribulations? You will remember that during the First World War its receipts and profits had rocketed. At the beginning of the Second World

War it seemed as if the same thing was going to happen again. The winter of 1939 into 1940 saw a sharp upturn in business. Perhaps it was a case of "Eat, drink and be merrie, for tomorrow . . .". At the annual general meeting held at the Clifton Hotel, Welbeck Street, London (the Langham could not be used as it had been hit in an air raid) on 18 December 1940, Cecil Page told the shareholders that business up until May 1940 (the month of the Dunkirk evacuation) had been excellent and receipts were £20,000 ahead of the first eight months of the previous year. Business then declined sharply and by the end of June there were only 20 guests. The Board had considered closing part of the hotel but this was not practical and when restrictions were put on visits to Eastbourne they had no alternative but to close the hotel completely. This happened on 20 July 1940 and as we have already seen the Burlington, Cavendish and Queen's followed suit shortly afterwards. The staff, of course, had to find jobs elsewhere, and the few permanent residents permanent residences elsewhere. Cecil Page and Sam Eeley had a large farewell sit-down tea with all the staff and Cecil Page was,

> much touched by the many expressions of hope for an early re-opening and desire to return to the service of the Grand.

Barbed wire was now placed along the front and the bathing machines were turned on to their backs and filled with sand. A machine gun post was placed on the top of the hotel and a 6 inch naval gun on top of the Wish Tower.

A small maintenance staff of eight was retained to keep the hotel aired and cleaned or deal with any emergency. In trying to decide whether to pay a dividend and if so at what level, Cecil Page told the shareholders of reduced rentals from the shops and of worries about maintenance of the hotel with no real income for the foreseeable future. Nevertheless the financial position was sound — investments stood at £6,745, cash at the bank was £1,000, the company owned the freehold of the hotel and a number of other properties and the shops were bringing in £2,200 in rents. The hotel had made a net profit of £4,480 and the Board felt able to recommend a dividend of 2% with the realisation that it would be the last for some time.

The closure had of course happened fairly rapidly and the Board had to decide what to do with its stock of wine and groceries. They were advised that the white wine would not keep and therefore sold it as well as some champagne and red wine that had reached maturity. These sales realised £2,000 and apparently showed a profit over cost. The groceries were also sold. The company farm of course lost its main customer but continued to operate. There was difficulty obtaining feed for the chickens and pigs but the farm manager, Mr Booth, managed it and also managed to find customers for the produce. The Board planned to grow as many vegetables as possible — in the national interest. In the autumn of 1940 the vegetable garden received a direct hit from a bomb and an incendiary bomb fell in the chicken run. The greenhouses were severely damaged and one of the houses that the company leased out was demolished.

Mr Gill, manager only since Sam Eeley's retirement in 1939, left the company's employment at the end of September and sadly died on 30 October 1940. John Cholmeley, who had succeeded his father as company secretary in 1926, took over as Acting Manager and moved from London to Eastbourne. Mr Murray, the Grand's famous chef, offered his services to the War Office and soon became a Lieutenant on the messing staff of the Western Command. Miss Lloyd, the Manageress, was appointed to a post supervising conductresses on London Transport. (You will remember that Cecil Page was involved with the London Transport Board and will probably have organised this job for Miss Lloyd though, if so, he did not claim credit for it to the shareholders.)

At the annual general meeting Cecil Page also remarked on the valiant efforts of the staff on the night of the bombing of the SS *Barnhill* and concluded by proposing the 2% dividend less income tax of 8s 6d (42.5p) in the £. (You will also remember that before the First World War income tax had been 1s 2d (6p) in the £ and that Page's father had been complaining about that.)

DEATH OF SAM EELEY

At the next annual general meeting back at the Langham in January 1942 Cecil Page had to report the sad death of Sam Eeley who had been knocked down outside his cottage at Polegate by a motor van. This truly was the end of an era, for Sam Eeley and his wife had done more than perhaps anyone to build the glittering reputation the Grand Hotel had enjoyed from 1910 to 1939.

THE HOTEL REQUISITIONED

During 1941 the hotel was requisitioned by the Government which had requested occupation within three weeks. This had caused considerable consternation. Where could all the furniture from 300 rooms be stored properly and safely within three weeks? A school was found but that was requisitioned too and then the empty Queenwood School was found. All the furniture was moved and stored within four weeks and St Vincent's Lodge, owned by the company, was also used for storage. The Government allowed the company to retain the ballroom and two storerooms to be used for storage and also the wine cellar and the laundry. The hotel's curtains had to be left where they were for blackout purposes. Cecil Page lamented the loss of these as he knew they would be difficult to replace. He also told shareholders that the hurried move meant that the furniture was stacked to the ceilings,

which cannot be other than detrimental to its condition.

Two of the caretaker staff went to Queenwood and one to St Vincent's Lodge to continue their caretaking role while Mr West who had been with the hotel as an engineer for 43 years was taken on by the Government department that had requisitioned the hotel to look after the lighting and heating. J.D. Wood and Company, the estate agent and valuer, was commissioned to negotiate compensation and other expenses with the Government.

Incidentally this report to shareholders was submitted to the Ministry of Information for approval. The following sentence was cut out by the censor,

> Up to date the hotel premises have fortunately suffered no damage from enemy action, and we can only hope that our good fortune will continue and that eventually our property will be returned to us without any undue damage.

The farm prospered during 1941 and produced a net profit of £431, in spite of a late frost which damaged the fruit and crops, and in spite of the multitudinous regulations that a war, and especially this war, always brings. The farm continued to make a profit throughout the war.

A report from William Booth, gives an excellent impression of what was happening there. It was written in April 1944, ie two months before D-Day.

> Present situation is that garden is in quite good order having had favourable weather for working land. Early potatoes (Arran Pilot and Eclipse) are planted and some main crop (Majestic) are in and about 5 acres in all will be sown as, with subsidy and a good crop, potatoes are profitable. Broad beans, Carrots, Turnips, Onions, Spinach etc. are in and just showing. Two sowings of Peas have also been made. Fruit trees have been pruned and given usual attention. Plums and Pears are just bursting into bloom. Some varieties of apple trees have very much deteriorated, Lord Derby and Worcester Pearmain are very bad. Soft fruit plantation is in a very bad state owing to lack of attention and age combined with disease, Big Bud in blackcurrants and dying back in Gooseberries. With the necessary

labour being assured it would pay to start an entirely fresh plantation next autumn or winter.

Greenhouses — Two are planted up with Tomatoes and a third almost finished. I have plenty of good plants to finish all houses. I had trouble early on with damping off which, after trying many remedies I was able to trace to a water tank which has now been attended to. There has been a fair crop of Lettuces in two houses and am pulling Radish from another. I hope to grow some cucumbers in Cloche as I shall use this as part of 10 per cent glass allowed for crops other than Tomatoes.

Stock — Have 16 pigs, weights between 5 and 10 score. They are all doing well but would do much better if I could get more food. My ration allowance is only 7.5 cwt. per month for Pigs and Poultry. Even when this augmented with every scrap of waste from the garden and 3 small lots of swill I collect it is not nearly sufficient. Have not been able to purchase any feeding potatoes in this district for months past.

Chickens — Have about 40 two year old birds and 40 pullets purchased last year which are just coming in to lay being very late hatched. Have three hens sitting being all the broodies I have at present. Have two cockerels with Light Sussex and Rhode Island and hope to hatch more as hens go broody.

Staff — We lost Marchant suddenly a month ago. He was a good all round man and it will not be possible to replace him. Besides feeding he was able to do any job as well as work machines. Read is able to look after most of the outside work but not the glass.

Ames — a youth of 18 very undersized and not fit for the services is capable of a fair day's work.

Beech — a youth who is not much good who will be called up for RAF next month [a good job the Battle of Britain was over].

Miss Jones — a land girl who has now been with us 3 weeks and is shaping very well. [Yes, but the Directors want to know what her work is like, Mr Booth.]

One part time woman working and two others I can call on. I also employ 2 civil defence workers when they are available. They are both good men and earn their pay, 1/3d [6.25p] per hour.

The rest of the hotel operations enabled the company to add several thousand pounds to its reserves. In 1943 it was felt necessary to sell the remaining wine stock and this realised just over £11,000. By the time of the annual general meeting in July 1945 (the company's year end had been changed from September to April) shareholders were naturally anxious to know when the hotel would re-open (VE — Victory in Europe — Day had been 8 May 1945). The Government however were not making any promises about when they would leave. Cecil Page was able to tell shareholders that he was making representations to his Member of Parliament and that he had also recently visited the hotel. It was at least structurally sound and had escaped any bomb damage. Nevertheless there was clearly a great deal of work to be done before it could possibly be opened again as a hotel and much would depend on the availability of workmen, materials and staff. He had already negotiated the appointment of a new manager — Flight Lieutenant Beattie who had been at the Queen's Hotel, Harrogate and at the Langham, Portland Place (where the company held its AGM).

WHAT WAS THE GRAND USED FOR DURING THE WAR?

Government departments are shrouded in secrecy at the best of times and during a war "careless talk costs lives". It has therefore been difficult to find out exactly which department used the Grand during the war and for what. It was said that the Germans planned to use the hotel as their headquarters in Southern England after their invasion in 1940!

What was certain was the fact that troops that went into Europe through Normandy in June 1944 were billeted at the Grand. Ben Johnson, who was in the 99th London Welsh Heavy Anti-Aircraft Regiment and went up the Normandy beaches on D-Day plus 3, remembers his time at the Grand in

Ben Johnson was stationed at the Grand — there were no carpets in those days.

Barbed wire defences — obviously some people managed to get through.

May 1944. He can remember the anti-aircraft guns on the front opposite the hotel and he can remember that there were no carpets in the hotel. He and his mates slept in sleeping bags on straw mattresses on the floor three or four to a room. He can also remember one or two dances (they must have been in the hall because if you remember, the company had been able to retain the Ballroom and use it for storage).

There were also American forces stationed at the Grand. Captain Arvo Haapa of the Army Corps of Engineers was billeted at the hotel, also in 1944. He married while in England and he and his wife spent part of their honeymoon in Eastbourne. They had met when they were both on the staff of the *Columbus Citizen* newspaper in Ohio and experienced some difficulty in gaining permission from the US Army to allow them to marry in England. In the end they achieved it and after their time in Eastbourne both went into Europe. Arvo in fact went as part of a small team — a Major, another Captain and five enlisted men — to run Hitler's Berchtesgaden. (Many of the personnel at the Grand were being trained to take over the running of towns in Germany once the country had been defeated.) Captain Haapa was part of a unit called First Civil Affairs Unit, European Civil Affairs Division — a name which was later, no doubt to the relief of everyone concerned, changed to American Military Government.

Eventually, and romantically, Arvo and his wife Mary spent 14 months in Berchtesgaden (in spite of its grim association with Hitler it is a beautiful town in the Bavarian Alps). They retraced their steps to Eastbourne and Europe as part of the 40th anniversary of the D-Day landings in 1944, and the current manager of the Grand Hotel laid on a real welcome for them. He also allowed them to stay in the hotel for the war-time price — £1 17s 6d (£1.87½p).

The Canadians who took part in the famous Dieppe Raid on 19 August 1942 also trained in Eastbourne. Jack Breach

Arvo Haapa — the American soldier who came back.

remembers that after the war the Corporation felt that the tie with Eastbourne was so strong they sent a book on Eastbourne during the war to 150 Canadian travel agents.

AN OUTSIDER'S VIEW OF WAR-TIME EASTBOURNE

Perhaps we should end this chapter with an outsider's view of Eastbourne during the war and then move on to happier days,

We came to Eastbourne from the North in early 1942. None of my unit knew anything about the town; very few of us had ever heard of it. It was our home for nearly two years until D-Day. Eastbourne in those days presented a queer mixture of its former splendour and its garrison activities. We noticed its wide, spacious streets, treelined with their grass verges now churned up by tank tracks. Camouflage nets hung from the trees. Initially we were very bored but the locals arranged many things — plays, films, dancing twice a week for 6d [2½p] and our own library scheme.

CHAPTER SEVEN

"WE DON'T WANT THE SAME KIND OF MEN LOOKING AFTER OUR AFFAIRS"

GREAT BRITAIN IN THE LATE 1940s

To the amazement of some, Winston Churchill and the Conservatives were swept from power in the "Khaki" election of 1945. The Labour Party won 393 seats against the Conservatives' 213 and 31 for the other parties. The war had brought about a general determination not to return to the bad old 1930s when the rulers, in this case the Conservative Party, were deemed to have got things badly wrong. The feeling was,

"We fought to save our country and now we, and not they, are going to run it".

Unfortunately for these splendid aspirations economic reality meant that whoever was running the country was in for a very difficult time. As soon as the United States defeated Japan in August 1945 the Lend-Lease Agreements were ended. Britain had lost many of her overseas investments during the war and much of her export trade. The raw materials and food she needed to import were scarce and expensive. It was going to be no easy task giving the people the goodies they thought they had earned. Rationing stayed in force until the 1950s. For basic food stuffs you needed coupons and for clothing, clothing coupons; tinned fruits and dried fruits were on one sort of points system and chocolate and sweets on another. In 1948 each person had a weekly allowance of 13 oz of meat, 1.5 oz of cheese, 6 oz of butter and margarine, 1 oz of cooking fat, 8 oz of sugar, 2 pints of milk and 1 egg. In July 1946 bread rationing was introduced and stayed in force until July 1948. That had not been necessary in the actual course of either the First or Second World Wars. Officially meals in restaurants were restricted to three courses and a price of 5s (25p).

This period of socialist government is most famous, not only for austerity personified by the ascetic Chancellor of the Exchequer Stafford Cripps, but also for its implementation of the first trappings of the Welfare State and for its nationalisation programme. The National Insurance Act was followed by the National Assistance Act and by the setting up of the National Health Service and these three between them meant the end of the appalling destitution that had been the lot of so many in the 1930s. The coal industry was nationalised as were the railways, road haulage, electricity and gas. British European Airways (BEA) and the British Overseas Airways Corporation (BOAC) took over most of civil flying. The Bank of England was formally nationalised and foreign exchange control was continued. The socialists were supposed to have control of the "commanding heights" of the economy. Actually what they had done was to get hold of some of the most inefficient and run-down parts of British industry and having got them left the same fuddy-duddy people running them. Instead of getting the economy right and making the cake bigger they concentrated on sharing out the cake which was crumbling anyway.

They also concentrated far too much on the Empire, a

mistake continued by their Conservative successors in the 1950s, and though they did rid the country of the burden of India, they spent many millions maintaining a presence in the Middle East, Far East and Africa which should have been spent on re-equipping industry at home.

THE GRAND HOTEL RE-OPENS

How would the Grand Hotel cope with this world of planning and regulations, of austerity and rationing, of restrictions on everything, of a maximum charge of 5s (25p) on meals?

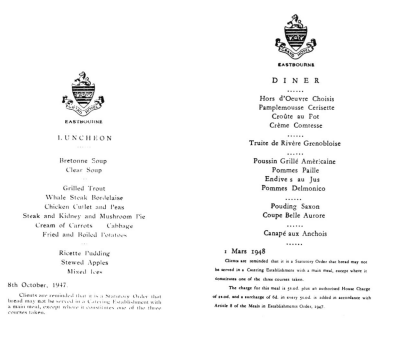

Menus from 1947 and 1948 which show the restriction on bread. All of this for 7s 6d (37.5p)!

First of all, the hotel had to be opened and that did not prove to be easy.

"We don't want the same kind of men looking after our affairs"

The company were in fact approached by the estate agent Horton Ledger who said that they had clients who were interested in buying the hotel. The Board did not pursue this offer although Sir John Laurie of stockbrokers, Laurie Milbank, wrote,

> My dear Cholmeley
>   We are getting client's enquiries about the Grand Hotel shares, and I shall be much obliged if you can give me any information.
>   You have doubtless heard of the bid being made from Brighton and in view of the very difficult state of affairs [sic] in general and the labour in particlar, it seems some time before you will be able to renovate the Hotel as you'd wish, should this be the case, the bidding seems very high.
>   Will you kindly send me three copies of your last report.

The hotel was handed back finally by the Government on 11 March 1946, ten months after victory in Europe and seven after victory over Japan. Dick Beattie, with his wife Betty, was ready

Dick and Betty Beattie — she was not to sing in the lounge!

to start as Manager. They had been interviewed at the Langham Hotel by one of the directors, Sir Roland Burke. Mrs Beattie was told that one of the conditions of employment was that she was not to sing in the lounge! Presumably either Mrs Eeley or Mrs Gill had done that.

Dick Beattie, born in 1911, had not followed his father into journalism where his father had enjoyed a successful career on the *Evening News* and *Daily Mail*. Educated at Sherborne and New College, Oxford, Dick began his hotel career as a trainee cook at one of the big London hotels. He then went to a hotel in Nice where he worked 14 hours a day for 15s (75p) a month and two free meals a day. He then became Assistant Manager of the Queen's Hotel at Hastings. After 15 months he went to Berlin as a reception clerk at a fashionable hotel used by all the top Nazis including Adolf Hitler in 1934. He then moved to Paris and towards the end of the 1930s became Manager of the Queen's Hotel in Harrogate. During the war after a short spell with the Army Catering Corps he joined the RAF and eventually became a pilot instructor.

Dick Beattie's opening salary was £550 and then, once the hotel opened, £700. This was less than Sam Eeley had been paid twenty or even thirty years before. It was a low salary for the responsibility especially as the war years had been, as all war years are, highly inflationary. Not that the Board were out of step. Everyone tried to take on staff after the war at the same salaries they had received before the war. Dick Beattie was provided with rooms in the hotel for himself and his family and was allowed 33⅓% discount on all wines and spirits consumed by them. He was given the power to hire and fire any

servant other than the Housekeeper, Assistant Manager, Chef, Chief Engineer, Head Waiter and Hall Porter.

He was allowed 21 days holiday a year and had to have the Directors' sanction for any purchase over £50 except on food, beer, spirits, minerals, cigarettes and farm stocks.

They set to and with the help of the local architect Hugh Hubbard Ford restored the hotel as best they could. John Cholmeley, or just Cholmeley, as Cecil Page called him wrote this splendid letter to a Mr Dumaresq,

> I note that you are making preparations to scythe the lawn in front of Queenwood.
>
> I would be glad if you would kindly arrange to have this completed within the next fortnight (or at the most, three weeks) as I shall require to utilise part of this for cleaning the Hotel carpets.

Little maintenance work had been carried out during the war and much of the equipment had been neglected. The entire hot water and central heating system had to be overhauled, the bell system had to be rewired and the lifts reconditioned (in the army you run up and down stairs, you do not use lifts). In the event with Ministry of Works restrictions the overhaul of the central heating system took until September. The Post Office, which had removed the switchboard and telephones in 1940, would only let the hotel have 60% of the telephones back. (1946 was a great year to try to open a hotel!) Dick Beattie remembers that when the carpets, beds and wardrobes came back from Queenwood trying to allocate them to the correct rooms was a nightmare. Although the room numbers had been written on the articles in chalk in 1941 the numbers had either faded or smudged. Mr Drury, who had been the hotel's carpet man, although in his seventies, came back to help, but with most rooms having free-standing basins, some single, some double, it proved a long and arduous task.

Finally all was ready and on 22 September 1946, the day before the hotel re-opened after more than six years, Dick Beattie sent the following memo to the senior staff,

GRAND HOTEL

D.A. Stroud, Esq	Miss Dyson
Miss I. Lloyd	Mr Faldo
Mr Monnier	Mrs Davies
L.G. Lawrence, Esq	Mr Reid
S.J. Peckham, Esq	Mr Pantoney
Miss Davies	Mr Rogers

I should like you to convey the contents of this letter to the members of your staff:—

During the period of rehabilitation many of the normal rules of Hotels have been unnecessary and, therefore, disregarded, but now that from tomorrow there will be visitors arriving in the Hotel I want you to remind the staff of them, they are:-

1) There must be no smoking while on duty in Public rooms, or where preparing or taking part in the preparation of Food and Drink.

2) All staff are to use the staff staircases only.

3) The staff are to use the staff lavatories.

I feel sure that with the co-operation of the staff we are commencing another era of prosperity in the days of the Grand Hotel Company, and under the system of pay that I have inaugurated there is a direct interest for every member of the staff in the prosperity of the Hotel, and that prosperity depends 90 per cent, on the staff.

I want the staff to be cheerful, willing, and pleasant with the visitors and remember that it is they who are the salesmen of the Hotel, and our future business depends to a great extent on them.

I wish you all good luck in the commencement of our work here, and I know that you will overcome the difficulties which will face us in the opening weeks owing to many of the working parts of the Hotel not being completed.

Finally, I want to say to you that this has been in the past a first class Hotel, and I am determined that in the future it will be a first class Hotel once again, and *we must give first class service.*

(Signed)

. . . .

Manager

Grand Hotel,
Eastbourne.
22.9.1946

You will note that the efficient housekeeper Miss Lloyd had been brought back from supervising conductresses.

Bill Stapley, who retired on 30 October 1986, forty years to the day after he had started as a waiter, remembers that he arrived for an interview earlier in October. All men leaving the army were given a green card which meant that any employer advertising vacancies had to see them. He was interviewed by the deputy manager, Mr Stroud, who held out little hope of a job,

You see all these things in the army but actually . . .

In the event, a few days later he received a telegram saying come now! Bill's first weekend was a school half-term and the hotel was very busy. At one stage he dropped an ice cream on the floor at which Captain Lawrence (who was actually Italian) drew himself up to his full height and announced,

this kind of thing cannot happen at the Grand Hotel.

THE FARM AFTER THE WAR

As the hotel struggled into life again the farm started to cause problems to the company. William Booth, who had been a great servant of the company, finally felt he had had enough and left at the end of 1945 leaving the farm rudderless for a time. As the new age of austerity dawned greater restrictions on animal feedstuffs were imposed than had been operating during the war. In his report to shareholders in July 1947 Cecil Page continued to talk of the difficulties while emphasising that the farm was a useful source of supply for the hotel.

The difficulties can perhaps be gauged by this letter from one of the farm employees,

12.4.47   1 Ocklynge Cottages
                                            Willingdon Road
                                            Eastbourne

Messrs Mayo & Perkins
1a Terminus Buildings
Eastbourne

Dear Sirs

In reply to your letter giving me notice to quit the Grand Hotel Cottage.

It appears the words I used to terminate my employment, have like everything else connected with the farm manager Mr Barratt, been distorted, apparently he realizes if he told the truth, it would be himself and not I who would be leaving. I have been most interested in my work, and am very sorry I had to end it this way, but after fourteen months of trying to cover his (Mr Barratt's) mistakes and lack of knowledge. I am tired of using my brain and energy to keep him in his job, and if the management of the Grand Hotel fail to see who has been running their farm. I shall be very pleased to get out of their employment and cottage, and can assure you I am doing everything in my power to do so.

Yours faithfully,
(signed) F.S. Catt

Cecil Page obviously found Barratt disconcerting. Dick Beattie remembers that when Page came down to Eastbourne on his monthly visit he would say to him, Dick Beattie, after going round the hotel,

Right, now let's go and see Beattie up at the farm.

THE FIRST WINTER AFTER THE WAR

As we have already seen the first winter after the war ended was not an easy time to be doing anything constructive and to make matters worse the weather was severe. The cost of everything had escalated sharply, particularly anything of quality and imported luxury items were just not available. Nevertheless, the Grand was open, if at this stage a pale shadow of its former self. Turnover was up but profits were not and the company was struggling to obtain its compensation from the Government. For the first time since the 1880s the balance sheet was not looking as healthy as it usually did. Cecil Page had not wanted to raise another debenture and the bank overdraft had risen to £81,436 (probably £1.2 million in today's terms). Mind you, the overdraft rate was 3.5% and the bank wrote regretting it could not be 3%.

Incidentally, Cholmeley resigned as secretary in 1946. Having addressed him as "Cholmeley" throughout his career Cecil Page relented and wrote to him as follows,

Dear Mr Cholmeley,

If it is your wish to resign following the Board Meeting on the 20th Sept. next, no doubt arrangements can be made by then for someone to take over from you.

Yours faithfully,

G.C. Page

For someone who had been secretary for 20 years, and with his father for 20 years before that, this seemed a little curt.

CONFERENCES

In his address to shareholders in 1947 Cecil Page mentioned that a number of successful conferences had been held. Before the war conferences had never been of significance for the hotel although in the post-war era as we shall see they were to become more and more significant. Many hotels in Eastbourne treated conference delegates as lucky extras. Indeed many of the 'city fathers' questioned whether the town wanted such people at all.

There were however those who tried to make Eastbourne attractive again to visitors. The carpet gardens, which had been

An aerial view of the hotel in the late 1940s — it had survived the war intact.

given over to the growing of onions during the war, became carpet gardens again. The Transport Department sliced the top off five buses, painted them white and organised trips along the front. Someone had the bright idea of giving them different names and this meant that the children wanted to go on all five. The "famous five" as they were known, were, The White Queen, The White Princess, The White Knight, The White Lady and The White Rabbit.

The Grand Hotel helped towards the promotion of Eastbourne by its efforts to bring conferences to the hotel and to the town. Perhaps Dick Beattie's greatest contribution to the Grand Hotel was his realisation that times had changed and that conferences were not only important to the Grand but actually vital for its continued existence.

Eastbourne's Carpet Gardens — they were used for growing onions during the Second World War.

THE ATMOSPHERE IN THE HOTEL IN THE LATE 1940s AND EARLY 1950s

In writing of the Grand Hotel from 1875 to 1945 we have had to rely on what people wrote down and annual reports. From 1945 we can rely on the memories of people who are alive and can talk of their time at the hotel. These memories can be vague at times and the story can become a little disjointed. Nevertheless the cumulative effect is to provide us with a view of the development of the hotel as it re-established itself as one of the country's premier hotels.

Dick Beattie was determined that he would be a hands-on manager just as Sam Eeley had been and he was not deterred by the reaction to his grand offer of a free bottle of champagne to the first guest who walked through the front door on that memorable sunny day, 23 September 1946,

No thanks, I don't drink.

Dick was to prove an able and, to his staff, fair manager. The hall porter, Ron Marion, who started in the hotel as a window cleaner in 1947 and who still worked as a hall porter in 1986, remembered that Dick would always cough to warn his staff that he was coming. Incidentally, Ron confirmed that the hotel was used as a training base during the war for people who went into the Control Commission in Germany after the war. Ron himself transferred from the Tank Corps into the Control Commission. After starting in the hotel as a window cleaner he became a night porter. The hours were fairly arduous — from 8.30 pm to 8.30 am 6 nights a week. During that time, once the bar shut at 10.30 pm it was the duty of the night porters to serve drinks and Ron remembered some heavy sessions, even the extreme moment when he found one intoxicated guest trying to set fire to the chairs in the lounge. The young hearties of the 1950s would constantly turn the lounge into an indoor rugby pitch using a cushion as the ball. When the game was finished and had been discussed until dawn, it was a walk up to Beachy Head to clear the tubes and then back for a hearty breakfast, including pints of Pimms.

The sticking of chamber pots on the Duke of Devonshire's head continued unabated and, of course, the standard trick of changing everyone's shoes around when they were put out for cleaning was done many times.

Ron's abiding memory of the 1950s' guest was that he was a conference delegate who came with his wife and played a lot of golf. The 1965 Labour Government budget damaged this trade, or certainly the wife part of it, by making business entertaining subject to tax. Ron could also remember the big card schools

The Duke of Devonshire with a chamber pot on his head — the standard adornment after a heavy night.

when the Jewish families from North London would come down for the holiday weekends. The men would play cards in the lounge, mainly bridge. Apparently the stakes were high though actual cash was rarely seen. Meantime the lonely wives upstairs were not averse to ringing the night porters for a gin and tonic. Ron was reticent on what the reward was for taking it up to them.

Ron clearly remembered the Bodkin Adams drama (more of that later). Adams, tried for murder in 1957 and acquitted after a sensational three-week trial, was a regular visitor to the hotel, both to look after residents (sick and wealthy old ladies were Adams' speciality) and to have his hair cut by Pickles the hairdresser. When Adams was arrested one national newspaper offered Ron £1,000 (perhaps £10,000 today) for his story. Ron declined but he and his fellow porters wrote to Adams in gaol wishing him well. Another of Ron's memories was of carrying

Leslie Jeffries out of the ballroom when he collapsed and died on stage in the middle of a performance of 'The Cat and the Canary'. You will remember that Leslie Jeffries had been the leader of the orchestra from 1934 to 1938. He returned to lead it again in 1946.

NIGHT-PORTER REPORTS

Every morning the night porters had to file their report of the night's proceedings in a book. This included the readings from clocks situated around the hotel so that the hotel could show their insurance company that the hotel was patrolled three times a night. The standard entry night after night would be,

20.30 — 2nd, 3rd, 4th porters on duty

00.20 — last guest retired
         rounds as per night watch clock
         bookings and medical calls nil

08.30 — all porters off duty

but occasionally there would be a more exciting entry as on the night of 30 November into 1 December 1967,

02.05 — Room 278 doubted the price of bottle of gin (£4.5s.0d). He was of the opinion I was trying to swindle him.

02.10 — I stopped serving drinks after I had to break up a fight in the lounge extension.

or on the night of 16 and 17 September 1969,

01.25 — Mr P. . . . . . W. . . . . (well known actor) telephoned regarding the heading on his account — Mr and Mrs P. W. . . . . . It appears that his wife needs assuring that he was on his own. This I can vouch for on the Friday night.

In August 1971 this entry appeared,

> 00.45 — Car MYO 625D's burglar alarm commenced to hoot.
> There were several complaints about the noise. As I didn't
> know the owner of the car there was nothing I could do
> except contact the police. They did their utmost to stop
> the noise but gave up after an hour. Eventually room 206
> phoned down and we discovered it was his car.

In early 1972 there was a slightly more exciting report,

> 00.10 — Mr Pait (4th night porter) shut Compton Street door on a
> girl that was insisting on seeing a waiter that sleeps in 14
> basement.
>
> 00.40 — The girl returned to the front entrance and made a scene,
> breaking the glass panel above the ramp. I called the police
> who took the girl away at 01.05 hours.

The local newspaper later reported,

> A 20 year old girl told Eastbourne magistrates yesterday that she
> visited the town to see her boyfriend. They had had a row and she
> started shouting and screaming. Suzanne Kurz, a housekeeper of
> Henley on Thames, pleaded guilty to being drunk and disorderly
> outside the Grand Hotel on 19 January. She was fined £1.

Plus ça change. Mrs Westwood, who worked as a maid in the
Grand from 1926 to 1928, can remember having a fight in the
women's dormitory with another girl over one of the waiters.
Although Mrs Westwood told the girl that she could have him,
she — Mrs Westwood — did in fact eventually marry him.

Mrs Westwood, incidentally, also recalls being chosen with
one of the other girls from the laundry to sell cotton-wool
snowballs at a Charity Ball at 2s 0d (10p) a snowball. She wore
high legged boots, a short white skirt and a silk top hat.

By the 1970s with real bombs exploding in British cities many
hotels were the subject of bomb scares and hoaxes. The night
porter's book reveals that two such hoaxes were played in 1972.
Drugs were also now more frequently heard about in Britain
and on the night of 28 and 29 July 1972,

00.45 — The police and 2 members of the drug squad searched room 16 basement for drugs but found nothing.

There were also some Hooray Henrys to contend with,

At 02.30 hours of 3/1/73 a car pulled up at the front doors and thinking they were residence (sic) the door was opened. They entered and sat opposite the porters' desk. They appeared to have been drinking. They were abusive in the use of language and asked for coffee stating that it was a 5 star hotel and demanding to be served. They were asked if they were residence and stated they were not using more abusive language asked for coffee. They were refused and shown the front doors.

And it was not only Hooray Henrys making a nuisance of themselves,

1—2/8/72: 00.20 — Three men and a woman stood on the front steps shouting anti-semetic (sic) slogans, I called the police and they attended to them.

The outdoor swimming pool, installed in 1962, was a regular source of complaint,

6—7/10/7
3: 03.10 — Lady Joseph (mother of Sir Keith Joseph) complained of noise from pool.

03.30 — Room 342 complained of same thing

but rather more dramatically

05.05 — Room 221 complained of noise above Room 332. Mr and Mrs McCrossman were having a dramatic row. The lady was screaming and had a bruise and a small cut behind the right ear. This I helped to clean up. The husband did not want me to call a doctor.

All in a night's work for the porters.

SIR SAMUEL AND LADY JOSEPH ————————

Talking of Lady Joseph, the ubiquitous Mrs Alice Riding, replacement for Miss Lloyd as housekeeper, kept details of the likes and dislikes of her regular visitors so that their rooms could be laid out as they wished and every idiosyncrasy catered for.

Thus for Sir Samuel and Lady Joseph there were four closely typed cards with all the details of how rooms 142, 143 and 144, plus bathroom, were to be laid out with plans on the back. This was followed by a page of extras to be installed (those items including some belonging to the Josephs were kept stored under the roof on the second floor opposite room 267). There were also some items kept by the engineers,

> 1 large convector heater for lobby
> "Light and Heat" lamp for bathroom ceiling
> TV extension flex for bedroom TV
> Small strip light for over long wall mirror in bedroom

Alice Riding — the ubiquitous replacement for Miss Lloyd (seated in the middle of the front row between Dick Beattie and Peter Hawley), on the occasion of her retirement in 1985.

This was followed by a page of details of how the beds were to be made up and then a page of special instructions such as,

No "eviction notice" on departure day

Does not mind shabby things, but everything washable or cleanable must be washed and cleaned for her arrival. (This also applies to her visitors.)

Every drawer, cupboard and wardrobe throughout suite must have new paper.

ALL CLEAN LINEN THROUGHOUT SUITE EACH DAY

Bath cleaner to keep and use cloths and gumption exclusively for her bathroom — not dettol in water

Valet NOT NIGHT PORTERS to clean shoes, even if they are put outside on the corridor. Shoes must be cleaned with NEUTRAL CREAM POLISH

DND (Do Not Disturb) NOTICES ON ALL DOORS PLUS 2 extra

Plenty of window wedges

Remove all buttermilk soap throughout the suite and put in large LUX soap

REMOVE ALL COATHANGERS THROUGHOUT SUITE (not forgetting cupboard in lobby)

Remove all correspondence folders, 'Know Britain', 'Grand Way of Life', 'The Good Life', matches, mending kits, Crinaline Lady.

USE ONLY 2-ply TOILET ROLLS (BABYSOFT, WHITE), remove Manilla (Bronco type) toilet rolls

REMOVE ALL ASHTRAYS — but put 2 square ones in 143

KEYS in envelope marked "Lady Joseph" left on writing table in 143 for her arrival containing

1 for Silverdale Entrance (loan her a submaster key)

1 for 143 writing table

1 for each of the chests of drawers in 142

Renew flowers in 143 on Tuesdays and Fridays

FIX A "PRIVATE" NOTICE TO OUTSIDE DOOR OF SUITE CORRIDOR SIDE

There was then a page on how the daily service was to be carried out. It seemed designed to make any but the most

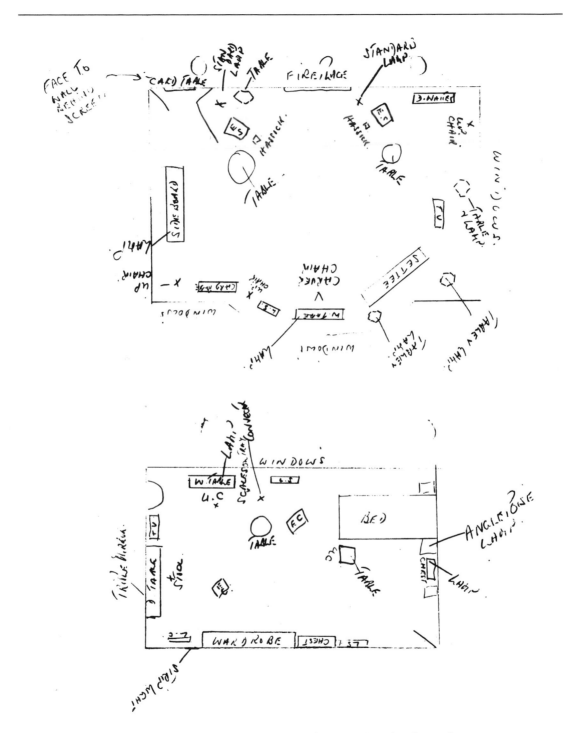

The plans of Sir Samuel and Lady Joseph's rooms kept by Alice Riding.

experienced maid extremely nervous. She would certainly need long arms.

MORNING SERVICE

No early morning tea or call

143 sitting room to be cleaned before 7.45 am each day (she listens to how long maid takes to do this). Draw curtains and change towels in 144 at same time.

DO NOT ENTER SUITE AGAIN UNTIL SHE RINGS FOR MAID (about mid morning)

MAID AND BATH CLEANER TO GO IN TOGETHER

Her two own hot water bottles to be emptied, thoroughly dried and placed under bedspread in 142

142 — bed to be turned down at 1.30 pm put in hot water bottle

EVENING SERVICE

Draw curtains in 144 and sitting room at 5.45 pm — all sitting room lights on at 5.45 pm

Room 142 — When turning down bed — bed clothes to be kept high up

Bedspread from 142 to be carefully folded and placed on bed R 144

Room 142 — Draw curtains when servicing room

2 hot water bottles to be filled at 8.30 pm very hot and three-quarters full (remove covers when filling and make sure bottles are dry and stoppers tight before putting in bed)

Room 144 — Tidied each night (look at wastepaper bin, basin and tumbler)

Bathroom — No evening service.

One cannot be sure what all that says about Lady Joseph but it certainly shows that the Grand was determined to try to look after its regular guests. In fact when Lady Joseph was ill in 1980 and could not leave London, Mrs Riding wrote to wish her well. Her son, Sir Keith, replied that,

She tells me of your responsibilities at the Grand and all the trouble you took to make her welcome. She still hopes to be able to come back to the Grand one day as she has a great fondness for it and all whom she knew there.

MYERS AND BENSON ————————————————

Perhaps the two most famous, or notorious, permanent residents of the Grand in the 1950s and 1960s were Myers and Benson. Wally Hawes, who was their chauffeur from 1955 until 1966 remembers them well. She was Mrs Beatrix Benson, though there was no sign of a Mr Benson, and he was her brother, Michael Lewis Myers. They were from a Jewish family of 12 daughters and one (the youngest) son. Mrs Benson saw it as her daughter's duty to protect the family fortune, currently in the hands of the only son, from the predatory gestures of any of the rest of the daughters or of any potential wife for Michael Myers.

They occupied the suite comprising rooms 112 and 114 with a bathroom in between and were eccentric beyond belief. They refused to have food from the dining room but would insist that a frozen chicken was bought every day at Sainsbury's. This had to be taken to their room for inspection. It then had to be cooked with a cup of water but no salt and placed in a casserole topped off with a covering of pastry so that no waiter could touch it. This continued for a year and they then changed to lamb cutlets which they had for the next year. Les King, the Grand's chef from the early 1950s into the 1990s, remembered this performance and remembered being called to the Myers/Benson suite at the end of each month and given a ticking off. He was however also given a cheque. The waiters and kitchen staff dreaded going to the suite. Over the years Les sent every single one until in the end the only person left was Dick Watson, the night baker. He lasted a fortnight before Mrs Benson said, inevitably,

That man's useless.

Les also remembered a niece of Mrs Benson coming to see her and remarking how thin she was. She then pulled down one of her eyelids, saw that her eye was red and exclaimed,

Aunty that's what poor people get when they're starving.

Myers kept a horse called George Henry for which Wally Hawes had to buy 2 lbs of carrots every day so that Myers could throw them in front of the horse as he took his daily ride. As they progressed up Southcliffe Avenue the carrots would roll behind the horse before it could pick them up. The residents complained about their carrot-strewn avenue and Wally was asked to pick them up in future.

Wally tells stories of how, when he drove them to London in their Rolls-Royce, known as "the flying hearse", they would always lie down in the back of the car and insisted on the tyre pressures being kept to 20 lbs per sq. in. and the speed restricted to 20 miles an hour. They would stop at a hotel just short of East Grinstead to use the lavatories but never bought a drink (they were teetotallers). Eventually the manager complained but back-tracked when he heard they were major shareholders of the hotel group.

Inevitably, in view of their eccentricity and irascibility bordering on paranoia, the staff played tricks on them. In view of Mrs Benson's views on her health Tony, the waiter, would put pepper up his nose so that he sneezed when he took in her lunch.

In spite of Mrs Benson's efforts to keep him alive Michael Myers eventually died and Hawes asking what to do with the horse was told to keep it until the weekend. Mrs Benson then advertised it in *Horse and Hound* asking £500 for it. Actually in Myers' will it said,

Any animals in my possession must be put down by laughing gas.

They do not make residents like that any more.

ECCENTRIC STAFF

Eccentricities were not confined to the guests. Dick Beattie remembered that one of his head waiters was taking considerable bribes from guests to make sure they sat at the dining tables they requested. He discovered this when there was a change and the new Head Waiter was told one Easter by a guest that he had paid his predecessor at Christmas to reserve a certain table.

The head receptionist for many years was Miss Winnie While who had come from a similar position at the Imperial Hotel, Harrogate. She was a miracle worker, able to get people rooms when the hotel was supposedly full. In the end she had to go as she was selling the rooms!

Lunch menu in 1954 — the choice has increased since 1948 and so has the price but it still looks staggeringly good value.

Everyone connected with the hotel at the time has his story of Doctor Bodkin Adams and Dick Beattie's was that on one of his regular visits to the hotel he bumped into him coming out of the lift. According to Dick he had just left a dead patient but Adams never mentioned it. Dick, not a man of socialist leanings, also liked to tell the story of the Electrical Trades Union Conference one year in the early 1960s. Apparently one of the delegates asked what the most expensive wine was in the hotel,

Chateau Yquem 1934.
We'll have that.
But it's a sweet wine for drinking with dessert.
Never mind. You said it was the most expensive so we'll have it.

And have it, apparently, they did, first drinking all the bottles and then all the half bottles.

On the subject of socialists Dick also remembered that Ernest Bevin, former dockers' leader, and ultimately Foreign secretary in Atlee's Government after the war, who was a regular at the hotel, got angry with him about a piece in a newspaper talking of Bevin staying at the Grand in a "6 guinea a day suite". (A working man's wage was about £3 a week at the time.)

When a hotel takes in thousands of guests over a period of time only the difficult or the funny ones stay in the memory. One particular insurance claim is instructive. In January 1955 a Mr Dennis Guest claimed damages against the hotel for food poisoning he claimed had come from oysters he had eaten at the hotel on New Year's Eve. The claim read,

Refund for dance tickets for Guest and Wife	£ 2.2.0
Extra farm wages 1-11 January	£ 5.5.0
Pain and suffering and for having a special evening's outing for himself and his wife spoilt	£26.5.0
Wife's expenses — travelling to hospital	£ 1.1.0
	£34.13.0

The claimant's solicitor went on to say that 18 months previously his client had eaten four and a half dozen oysters at one sitting without any ill effects. This particular claim was eventually settled for ten guineas for the claimant and four guineas for his solicitor. (Those were the days!)

A more tragic case concerned one of the hotel's kitchen porters, a Welshman called Davies, in 1949. Davies had a girl friend in a cafe in Terminus Road. She wanted to finish the relationship, perhaps because she had a husband serving in the army in Germany. Davies was very upset and got drunk. He then took a blunt table knife and went to the cafe. A scuffle followed and he stabbed her in the eye. He was charged with grievous bodily harm and then, when she died, with murder. There seemed little doubt that he had not meant to kill her but in English law if you attack someone with intent to do physical injury and that person dies the charge becomes murder. At the trial at Lewes assizes, after the shortest jury retirement in English legal history, Davies was found guilty, sentenced to death and hanged.

There was a certain amount of murder and suspected murder intertwined with some of the characters at the Grand in the 1950s. Wally Hawes, the Benson and Myers chauffeur, was called to jury service one year and although Myers immediately told him to write and say he could not go, Wally was not excused and sat on the jury of a double murder trial. The case was of a German who involved himself with a girl other than his wife. He was also tried at Lewes Crown Court and was in fact the last man to be hanged in England. Wally made the mistake of telling Myers that the money he received from the court for his expenses and loss of earnings was £2 more than Myers paid him. Guess who demanded he give up the £2?

BODKIN ADAMS

The most famous trial of the decade was that of Dr Bodkin Adams, the Eastbourne doctor who was beloved by his patients, mostly rather elderly widows with healthy bank balances. As the 1950s progressed and more and more of these widows died, often remembering Adams in their will, so the

Dr John Bodkin Adams — the longest murder trial in England this century.
(Photograph by courtesy of the BBC Hulton Picture Library.)

gossip spread. Indeed, there was a poem in circulation among a select group that went like this,

> In Eastbourne it is healthy
> And the residents are wealthy
> It's a miracle that anybody dies;
> Yet this pearl of English lidos
> Is a slaughter house of widows —
> If their bank rolls are above the normal size.

If they're lucky in addition
In their choice of a physician
And remember him when making out their wills
And bequeath their Rolls Royces
Then they soon hear angel voices
And are quickly freed from all their earthly ills.

If they're nervous or afraid of
What a heroine is made of
Their mentality will soon be reconditioned
So they needn't feel neglected
They will shortly be injected
With the heroin in which they were deficient.

As we witnessed the deceased borne
From the stately homes of Eastbourne
We are calm, for it may safely be assumed
That each lady that we bury
In the local cemetery
Will re-surface — when the body is exhumed.

It's the mortuary chapel
If they touch an Adam's apple
After parting with a Bentley as a fee
So to liquidate your odd kin
By the needle of the bodkin
Send them down to sunny Eastbourne by the sea.

Eventually the police pounced but almost unbelievably they charged him with the murder of the 81 year old widow Mrs Alice Morrell, six years before, and ignored the subsequent dubious cases. On a technical point concerning morphia Adams was acquitted after a sensational trial that occupied the front page of every national newspaper for three weeks. Lasting for 17 days it was the longest murder trial in England this century. The presiding judge was Mr (later Lord) Justice Devlin. The Attorney General, Sir Reginald Manningham Buller QC, was the prosecuting counsel and Geoffrey Lawrence QC the defence counsel. Adams was struck from the medical register but in 1961 was permitted to practise again and continued to do so in Eastbourne until his death in 1983.

In spite of the malicious gossip many in Eastbourne speak of Adams, with his soft Ulster accent, with great affection. Jack Breach and Leonard Earp both have personal experience of his good doctorship concerning their own families. Bill Stapley, who served as a waiter, and was ultimately Head Waiter, from 1946 until 1986, remembers that one day in the 1940s, Bodkin Adams was served a meringue Chantilly with synthetic cream in the hotel restaurant (a meringue Chantilly should of course have fresh cream but in the immediate post-war years it was unobtainable). Adams left the sweet on his plate, tore the menu in half, wrote on one half, "This shaving cream is unfit for human consumption", and stuck it into the sweet.

CHAPTER EIGHT

TIMES ARE CHANGING

THE WORLD WAS CHANGING————————————

In the late 1940s and early 1950s most of the civilised world was concentrating on picking up the pieces after six years of catastrophic war. Much of Europe had been utterly devastated and there was now an "Iron Curtain" down the middle of it with those on the Eastern side not likely to see the other side of it for many years if ever again. It was still possible to think that the same upper classes that ruled the Western world would continue to do so and indeed they did. The difference now was that even these classes were relatively impoverished by swingeing, some would even say confiscatory, taxation. The days of cheap domestic servants and very low wages were gone and the numbers who could afford the type of service offered by the Grand Hotel had dwindled dramatically. There were enough prosperous people still to fill the hotel at Easter, Whitsun and Christmas and initially in July and August too. But as the 1950s progressed so too did the competition from resorts overseas in the South of France, in Italy and Spain and they of course could guarantee the one thing you can never rely on in England — warm and sunny weather.

Furthermore the social climate was at last changing in England. Other classes besides the traditional upper classes began to assert themselves. At last the country as a whole began to prosper again, thanks partly to the loosening of controls by the Conservative Party, which regained power in 1951 and partly to the terms of world trade turning in the country's favour after the end of the Korean War in 1953. It was not the dynamic growth enjoyed by other western countries but we were gradually buoyed up by the growth of international trade even if our share of it was declining. On the back of this new prosperity the young of all classes started to assert themselves more whether it was the Teddy Boys of the working class or the more middle class groups of CND or skiffle and rock 'n roll. This was the era of 'Rock Around the Clock,' of Bill Haley, Tommy Steele and Lonnie Donnegan. It was the era of coffee bars, of *Room at the Top* and *Look Back in Anger*. The exciting things were now being done by the young and perhaps young middle-aged from every social class. It seems difficult to believe now that in 1959 when Penguin Books were on trial for obscenity for publishing *Lady Chatterley's Lover* that the prosecuting counsel could hold the book up in court and ask the jury — twelve honest burghers of London — whether it was the sort of book they would like their servants to read.

THE GRAND ADAPTS

Unfortunately perhaps there were now not many servants around and the Grand would have to adapt and keep on adapting if the hotel was to survive let alone prosper. In the 1950s Dick Beattie had realised that the small American Bar at the back of the hotel could not cope with his new conference business and the new bar was built (there had been a library

The new bar — the old American bar at the back of the hotel could not cope with the conference trade.

The sun lounge — bright in the daytime and warm and comfortable for dancing in the evening.

there before). The sun concourse was built — at the unbelievably low cost of £15,000 and also the new lounge on the left as you enter the hotel. The Compton Street entrance was closed and the reception area moved to where it is now. Before the concourse was built guests could only reach the Princes Room by going outside or through the kitchens.

By the early 1960s, as even the busy month of August was not so busy, Dick made some drastic changes. Perhaps spurred on by the marriage of his daughter Susan to the former cricket captain of Sussex, Hubert Doggart (for which event incidentally the splendid Myers lent his Rolls and Wally Hawes), he changed the image of the Grand as fast as he could.

In came the management consultants, Personnel Administration (PA) who recommended the following alterations,

a replanned kitchen
    — it had been unaltered for 40 years

changes in management
    — Beattie to have two assistant managers, one for catering
        and one for housekeeping
    — cashiers and receptionists to be interchangeable
    — general food store to be directly under the chef

the results apart from greater efficiency were,
    — wages overall were reduced by 4%
    — catering wages were reduced by 7.5%
    — laundry costs were reduced by £1,000 a year

Outside Dick turned the tennis court in the south-west corner of the garden, where the immortal Fred Perry had played into an open-air swimming pool. It was opened by the comedian Kenneth Horne and the Olympic champion Judy Grinham. In his instructions for the day to the staff Dick produced the unforgettable line,

2.35 to 2.40 pm Mr Horne invites Miss Judy Grinham to open the pool by diving into it.

The new pool — "Mr Horne invites Miss Judy Grinham to open the pool by diving into it."

This was on 21 May 1963 and in May 1964, Brian Johnston, the well-known cricket commentator and host of 'Down Your Way', who had spent his honeymoon at the Grand Hotel, opened a new games suite. The rooms included amongst other things table tennis tables and these were christened by the former world champions Johnny Leach and Diane Row.

CHANGE OF STYLE IN MUSIC

Dick also felt it was time to change the style of music. It was not so many years since the *London Evening Standard* had written in October 1953 that the Light Programme Director Kenneth Adam had moved the Grand Hotel music hour from 7.30 to 9 pm because it was affecting church attendance.

> Whenever the BBC have tried to drop this light music marathon they have been abused by every kind of listener from choleric colonels to irate ironmongers. Grand Hotel is the programme the BBC DARE NOT take off.

In 1955 the pianist Jack Byfield had returned to the Grand in place of Sydney Ffoulkes to play under Leslie Jeffries. He said at the time,

> This will be a Mecca of good music. We will supply what discerning people recognise as good music.

But as we have already seen the country's tastes were changing and after Jack had left after an acrimonious exchange of letters with Dick Beattie in 1959, Dick appointed the Harold Turner Four to play dance music every weekday from 8.30 until 11pm and from 8.30 to midnight on Saturdays in the Sun Lounge. No more worrying about the wonderful acoustics in the Lounge Hall now. It was the dancers Dick wanted. The charges were —

Monday to Friday	- dance	- 5s (25p)
	- dinner and dance	- 21s (£1.05)
Saturday	- dance	- 7s.6d (37.5p)
	- dinner and dance	- 21s (£1.05)

Nothing could more have signalled the 'wind of change'. *The Sunday Times* wrote on 10 March 1963,

Wind of change in Palm Court
It's goodbye to all that (and about time, too, for me) so far as the Grand Hotel and the Palm Court Orchestra is concerned. When I dropped into the Grand Hotel, Eastbourne, last week I found armies of workmen in overalls swarming all over the place, hard at work smashing the genteel Albert Sandler image that has made the Grand famous.

The Grand caught up with the times last autumn when the managing director, Mr Richard Beattie, found that customers were staying away in August, the peak month of the season. The first people to feel the wind of change were the Grand Hotel trio, last survivors of the days when schmaltzy music among the potted palms really drew the crowds. The trio leaves in June: a dance band takes over.

"Oh, yes," says Mr Beattie happily, "the change caused a little outrage among the elder residents." But worse was to follow. Management consultants from Personnel Administration Limited (the firm that did the work for the Royal Commission on the Press) were called

Les King in his kitchen – he was the maestro from the 1950s until 1991.

in and have been camping in the Grand for the last year. The leisurely atmosphere has gone for good.

The old-fashioned kitchens (unchanged for thirty-five years) have been redesigned, a £1,500 dishwasher installed. A heated swimming pool costing £25,000 is being dug right outside the main entrance with heated sea-water and an open-air cocktail terrace.

But, cruellest thrust of all for the (mostly) elderly guests, is a teenagers' games room with juke box, Coca-cola machine, dart-board and a pile of twist records "which", says Mr Beattie, "may be played all night as far as I am concerned."

The big idea is to persuade younger people to come to the Grand, and for families in their forties to bring teenage children. "The sort of people," says Mr Beattie, "who don't really dig Albert Sandler and all that stuff."

The *Daily Mail* joined in three months later, writing,

HEP
From Glyndebourne I went to the Grand Hotel Eastbourne, the original home of radio's Palm Court Orchestra, remember?

The old ladies and their poodles (7s6d a day for dogs) are still there talking about lumbago and the weather. But who can blame them for

Dick Beattie — "We are trying to be . . . um . . . what you call, with it" (with the Chairman, Plummer and a long-serving employee, Brooks).

looking a little suprised these days? The place is getting hep, real hep, man.

Yes, says the Managing Director, Richard Beattie, 'We are trying to be . . . um . . . what you call with it.'

I did find just one potted palm, but it was hidden behind a hydrangea. The Palm Court has gone. So has the tennis court where Fred Perry used to play.

Yesterday they opened a brand new swimming pool where Perry played. A piano shaped affair, as a slight concession to the hotel's history. They keep the original piano too. But they have canned music coming over the loudspeakers.

And in the basement they are installing a soda fountain. And a juke box. Yes, a juke box in the Grand Hotel, Eastbourne.

The *Daily Mail* followed this up in July 1963 with the following,

The discordant note struck in the Palm Court of the Grand Hotel yesterday came from an Hawaiian shirt whose lines were almost audible. The wearer got no reproof, which would have been swift and certain not long ago, from the manager. In fact, he WAS the manager.

Dick Beattie was determined to pull the hotel away from the cathedral calm of the Palm Court and emphasised the light and airy extension with its four piece swinging combo overlooking the open-air pool. He was full of praise for the holiday camp king Billy Butlin,

> The man is a genius. People in this country are Butlin minded. Why? Because when they are on holiday he gives them something to *do*.

My goodness, we have come a long way from the Grand Hotel of Cecil Page and his father, Ernest. Cecil never had to witness these changes as he died in 1960.

Dick Beattie continued,

> To beat the competition of foreign holidays we are all going to have to do more than be good hotels, with good food, service and comfort. Our seaside hotels to survive are going to have to do something like this. If they don't they'll go bankrupt. The 'grand' hotels used to scare off some people who could well afford to stay at them. Holidaymakers nowadays insist on an informal atmosphere and handy 'with-it' entertainment.

The hunt at the Grand — the right image?

They don't want the subservient service of old. They don't want rules and regulations. Come to that we have cut ours down to one — a tie at dinner, please.

They want to see that hotels have moved beyond the '30s. If that girl — he nodded towards a pretty thing in a bikini — walked through the lounge, it wouldn't bother me in the least.

GRAND HOTEL'S BECKSTEIN STOLEN

The hotel's famous Beckstein was in fact stolen during the 1950s. Gordon Platt, secretary at the Grand, remembers it well. The thief apparently was the son of a successful musical instrument retailer in the Midlands. He had apparently not run his father's business successfully and had become a piano broker. In the course of this business he stayed regularly both at the Savoy Hotel in London and at the Grand. Gordon remembers that he was a little slow at settling his bills but always did so in the end.

One afternoon Gordon's telephone rang and it was the police enquiring if the hotel had a piano for sale. It transpired that the thief had taken the number of the Grand's Beckstein and gone to one of the department stores and told them he could get them a Beckstein No. so-and-so. They had negotiated and the store, presumably knowing the man, had agreed to pay him in advance. The thief had then disappeared and when no piano had arrived the store had contacted Beckstein who had told them that particular piano was at the Grand Hotel. The man was eventually arrested and went to gaol for 18 months.

The story had a strange sequel. The thief at the time of his arrest owed the Grand £200 but he had also left a suitcase there. After about a year Gordon received a telephone call from Malcolm (later Sir Malcolm) Sargent enquiring whether they had the suitcase. When he was told yes he requested its release but was informed of the £200 bill outstanding. Sargent offered to send £100 for the suitcase telling Gordon that the thief's father had given him his first chance and he wanted to repay the debt by setting up the son when he was released from gaol.

BRITAIN IN THE 1960s

We have already seen that society was changing in Britain and in the 1960s the pace accelerated. Relative to other Western countries Britain's poor economic performance continued and the decade was punctuated regularly with sterling crises and deflationary budgets. The socialists' answer to this — Harold Wilson and a Labour Government were elected in 1964 after 13 years of Tory rule — was heavy and discriminatory taxation. It discriminated against the Grand's traditional customers — Capital Gains Tax, tax on company entertaining, no tax relief on overdrafts. In 1966 after a long seamen's strike — strikes were about to become a daily part of British life — followed by the inevitable pressure on the pound, the Labour Government introduced a severe credit squeeze in July 1966 (many of the population barely noticed as England was in the process of winning the World Cup). The traditional customers of the Grand noticed however and this period saw the final break from the old type of customer to the new.

CONFERENCES

Renewed effort was expended on winning business. In the Conferences and Exhibitions magazine Dick Beattie took an advertisement headed,

CONFERENCE ORGANISERS
Write your own cheque (up to £1,500)
a remarkable offer by one of Europe's leading hoteliers
Follow the new trend towards conferences in January or February

when the entire unhurried resources are available at rates which could mean in effect that every fifth delegate attends free of charge. On a 5 day booking for 300 delegates you could save as much as £1,500.

Facilities — acoustically perfect conference rooms
                seating from 50 to 350
                separate work study rooms
                lavishly equipped conference office
                closed circuit TV
                technical equipment for complete floor shows

Over the years the hotel has provided some special items for the conference delegates — a wrestling evening in a full-size wrestling ring; the Royal Marines Band; a baby elephant for a medieval evening where it drank the mead from the jugs through its trunk and showed no mercy to the delegates from the other end of its anatomy.

EXPANSION

As well as trying to woo the conference delegates the hotel sought expansion into other hotels. In 1954 the company had sold the farm. It had been a constant source of trouble since the war — Cecil Page had got into the habit of saying whenever he visited it, "What major disasters have there been since last time?" — and as the freezers and the mass growing of farm produce made it more and more uneconomic, the Board decided to sell it. The 18¾ acres were sold for £19,500 (the solicitors' charges incidentally were £88 15s 0d) to New Ideal Homesteads and permission was given to erect 6 detached dwelling houses, 20 detached bungalows and 74 semi-detached bungalows. Mrs Hazel Reigate, who lives in one of the detached bungalows, has traced the history of her house,

The first owner in November 1955 paid £2,400 — there was no garage then

Barry and Alan — two page boys in the 1950s.

> The second owner paid £4,500 — including a garage
> She paid £21,950 in 1979
> She has since added a two-room extension, conservatory and central
>   heating and the house is now valued at £55,000.

On the face of it the £19,500 that the Grand sold the land for in 1954 seems a giveaway but anything to do with property always does a few years later. It was a significant sum then (you will remember that Ernest Page had appreciated in 1918 when the company had bought the farm that the land would be easily saleable for development) and the company could find ways of using the cash.

The sale of the farm was part of a move away from the self-sufficiency of the early 1950s when Dick Beattie had put together again the town within a town in which every need could be accommodated. Apart from all the services and comforts offered by a luxury hotel, the Grand could boast its own farm, its own gardens, its own laundry, its own garage, its own carpenters, its own engineers, its own upholsterers and its own valets and maids. In the writing room the hotel even used to mix its own inks, red and blue. (The pens incidentally came from the hotel stores in two parts, the holders and the nibs.) As if to emphasise its self-sufficiency and importance the hotel flag was raised on the hotel roof every morning and lowered at dusk. (When this practice was discontinued and the flag was left flying permanently the hotel quickly received a complaint from a retired colonel living in Eastbourne protesting about the lowering of standards.) Needless to say someone also raised the flag the wrong way up one day and the telephone never stopped ringing until it had been changed.

One of the ways that the money was used was in buying the Manor House at Leamington Spa in Warwickshire. (Dick Beattie told the story that Cecil Page, when he went to visit it, got on the train and went to Woodhall Spa in Lincolnshire.) This move led on to the building of the de Montfort at nearby Kenilworth. In fact neither of these moves showed much logic except perhaps as the beginning of a general expansion into a group of hotels throughout the country. This was to happen, but not under the sole leadership of the Grand Hotel, for in January 1967 the company received a takeover offer from De Vere Hotels.

THE DE VERE GROUP

The De Vere Group had been built up by Leopold Muller and Leslie Jackson. Leopold Muller had owned his own large meat canning business in Czechoslovakia before the war but had been advised to flee the country when the Nazis arrived in 1938. His strengths in the hotel business related to the kitchen. He was a master butcher and once established in this country set up his own commissary in Smithfield Market. He brought his own beef down from Scotland after which it was always hung for 14 to 17 days (that is why the beef at the Grand is so delicious).

Leslie Jackson first met Muller when Muller owned the Oxford Street Restaurant, and Jackson, an accountant, audited his books. Together they bought the Chicken Inn in the Haymarket and opened other Chicken Inns. They were in the fast-food business in the 1950s when it was not the fashion it became later. In 1956 they bought the hotel group Spears and Pond which included the Grand Hotel Scarborough, the Grand Hotel Brighton, the Queen's Hotel Eastbourne, Bailey's Hotel Gloucester Road London, the Calverley Hotel at Tunbridge Wells and the Royal Clarence at Exeter.

In 1959 Muller and Jackson accepted a bid from Express Dairies for Spears and Pond and in 1960 broke away and bought the De Vere Hotel in Kensington. They expanded rapidly and went public in 1965. One of the hotels they had bought was the Cavendish in Eastbourne — bought in fact from the two surviving spinsters of the famous Pimms family. They now wanted to establish a commanding presence in the "conference" towns, and recognising the Grand Hotel's expertise in this area made an offer for the company's shares. The original offer was 9s (45p) a share valuing the company at £700,000. (The *Chronicle* was so excited it printed that the offer was £7 million!) To begin with the Board rejected the bid but when it was raised to 9s 6d, i.e. another £40,000, they recommended acceptance. They could not in fact have resisted the bid as ownership of the shares was very widespread and the Board themselves (G.W. Plummer — Chairman; T.I.S. Eeley — one of Sam Eeley's sons; R.E. Huffman — an ex-Unilever director; Dick Beattie and Gordon Platt — joint Managing Directors) had no significant stake.

Within a few months the whole Board had resigned and were replaced by Leopold Muller, Leslie Jackson and Reg Constable. The new Board immediately set about spending money on the hotel and one of the first things they did was to paint the outside white. Before it had been grey stone. This painting now has to be done every six years and according to Bill Gregory currently costs £100,000. (Bill Gregory has been concerned with maintenance at the Grand since it re-opened after the War and has recently been promoted to Estates Manager, Southern Region, De Vere Hotels.) Out went the old free-standing furniture and in came fitted furniture. Out went the lifts in the East and West Wing and in came more rooms with bathrooms. The hotel had lost its AA 5-Star rating in 1965 but this was restored after De Vere had spent £750,000 (perhaps £4.5 million today) between 1965 and 1971. The long-established laundry was finally closed down. The health inspector had not liked it since the building of the concourse in the 1950s had blocked out its light and ventilation. The De Vere Board did not like it because of its cost. Savings of 30% were achieved by contracting out the laundry.

A major reason for the AA's downgrading of the hotel in 1965 had been the low number of bathrooms. By 1970 all 200 rooms had a private bathroom. The new management also put in two miles of carpets upstairs, lowered many ceilings in public rooms and completely refurnished all the bedrooms. 15 luxury suites were created including a penthouse suite. Bed and breakfast rates were now £5 to £8 and inclusive terms £7 to £10.

PERMANENT RESIDENTS

We have already seen that the notorious Myers and Benson were permanent residents and terrorised the staff daily. Until the 1960s there were many other permanent residents. Below is a list of those in residence in September 1960 with details of what they paid.

RESIDENTS' TERMS

Apt.	Name	Present	Proposed
206/207	R.M. BLAIR	25 guineas Apartments Lunch 12/6 Dinner 15/- 6 months' notice	27 guineas Apartments Lunch & Dinner at Hotel Prices
213/4/6	W.H. FOSTER	£5/15/6 per day	£6/6/- per day
208/9/10	LADY HANSEN	£6/6/- per day Guests in suite 45/- Guests not in suite at minimum tariff	£7/7/- per day Guests in suite 55/- Guests not in suite at minimum tariff for period
139/40/41	E.S. HUNTER	£4/17/6 per day Guests in suite 45/- Not in suite 50/-	£5/10/- per day Guests in suite 55/- Guests not in suite at minimum tariff for period
6/7	C.E. LEMAN	£3/15/- per day	£4/-/- per day
111	D. LEVENE	£3/3/- per day	£3/10/- per day
112	MRS BENSON	£3/13/6 per day	£7 per day
113/4/6	M. MYERS	£6/6/- per day	£7 per day
234	LADY PRINCE	£3/13/6 per day	£4/-/- per day
108/9/10	MR & MRS KINNEAR HALL	£8/18/6 per day	£9/9/- per day
349	MRS PYPER	£2/12/6 per day	£3/-/- per day
106/107	MRS PEARSON	£6/6/- per day	£6/16/- per day
196/7	MRS WILSON	£4/14/6 per day	£5/-/- per day

Total increase £6/10/- per day
£2,272 per year

12.9.60.

As the 1960s progressed the hotel decided that permanent residents were not a paying proposition and as they left for one reason or another no new ones were taken on. By 1965 the number was down to nine and by 1971 the only two left were

Mrs Benson and Sir George and Lady Williamson. It would seem that Lady Williamson could be as big a tartar as Mrs Benson. Here is a letter she wrote to Mr Dumhoff. (Mr Dumhoff was not Lady Williamson's pet name for the Manager but was in fact the reception manager. He was eventually sacked for ordering £4,000 of waiters' order pads. The hotel is still using them twenty years later.)

Dear Mr Dumhoff,

My husband spoke to you yesterday re. gratuities which are supposed to be for service (and we only got our Breakfast on Sat. after *three* ringups to floor service and it eventually arrived nearly 20 minute late after all sorts of different excuses).

Naturally we do not feel like tipping those responsible for service like that — or rather *lack* of service.

However the Bill has just arrived and we note we are charged the *full* Gratuities.

Personally we consider this "pistol point" tipping a great mistake and would much rather do our own individual tipping to members of the staff, such as waiters and bedroom maids from whom we get good service.

Yours etc.

(Lady) L. Williamson

P.S. Also charged a phone call which we did not have.

The permanent residents were a law unto themselves. Major Blair was a stickler for protocol and would not allow a porter to travel in the lift with him. His sarcasm could fell the chef at a hundred paces,

You can tell what's on the menu by what the orchestra's playing.

The permanent residents were given one section of the dining room and an old waiter to look after them. He would often order for them without even consulting them. Bill Stapley remembers when Lady Prince ordered a 'honeymoon' melon and Mrs Pearson, who was a little deaf, proclaiming in a loud voice,

I think this fish is a bit off.

(This was followed by an avalanche of cancellations for the fish.)

Another permanent resident, who was blind and was a stickler for time (she had a braille watch), was waited on one night by her waiter in his sou'wester — he had been late cycling in from Hampden Park in torrential rain.

Mrs Pyper was found dead drunk in her bath one night fully clothed. No doubt she would have been good company for Mrs Davenport's son with his pint of gin each morning. Mrs Davenport herself seemed disinclined to look after her health. Her doctor felt there was too much fat around her heart and suggested fruit and salad. Mrs Davenport continued to eat her enormous meals and added the fruit and salad! Then there were Mr and Mrs Kinnear Hall who complained they were given Carlsberg when they asked for a lager. Is there no British lager? Soon after this complaint they were seen climbing into their large Mercedes.

Mr and Mrs Brodie James were great ones for routine and order in their lives. The porters were required to wear gloves to put logs on their fire and in the dining room every morning without fail Mr Brodie James would say,

In the right hand cupboard you will find some All Bran . . .

One day, the waiter Gordon Morris found some weevils in the All Bran. When he pointed this out to Brodie James he said in his measured tones,

Do you know, Morris, you've probably saved my life?

Then there was Mr Hunter, an old man with a beard and a stick. He was constantly visited by young girls and was known to the staff as "shagger".

FAMOUS GUESTS AT THE GRAND

While the general clientele of the hotel gradually changed after the war nevertheless the rich and the famous still came. War heroes Viscount Montgomery of Alamein and Field Marshal Slim came, as did Lord Tenby and Harold Macmillan. Macmillan was later to tell the British people they had never had it so good. Let us hope he felt that way about his stay at the Grand.

Harold Macmillan.

Dick Beattie remembers the visit of Harold Macmillan — he had married the daughter of the Duke of Devonshire and therefore had some connection with Eastbourne — and that when he took Mr Macmillan to his suite, the Prime Minister came out with the "Do not disturb" sign and asked if he could take it to Downing Street.

We have already seen that Ernest Bevin came when he was Foreign Secretary and with him he brought his scrambler telephone.

Gordon Morris remembers saying to Bevin when Bevin was talking glowingly about the water being sprayed into the pits to keep down the dust level,

Do you realise this will give the miners arthritis?

Bevin aghast replied,

My advisers never told me about that.

Princess Margaret came at the age of 17 and had a lunch party with the Dukes of Norfolk, Devonshire and Richmond, and the Mayor of Eastbourne. The Duke of Edinburgh also came and Princess Alexandra — Dick Beattie was struck by how tall the Princess was.

From the world of show business Anna Neagle came, as did Pete Murray, the famous disc jockey of the 1950s and 1960s and also the comedian, Stanley Baxter. Omar Sharif, star of *Lawrence of Arabia* and *Dr Zhivago* came to indulge his passion for bridge and played in one of the bridge unions. Oliver Reed came and enjoyed a breakfast of two boiled eggs and two half bottles of champagne. Also from the world of show business came Alec Guinness, star of *Bridge over the River Kwai* and so many post-war British films. From television there came Jimmy Saville, the brilliant presenter of 'Top of the Pops' and 'Jim'll Fix It', Des O'Connor, Jimmy Tarbuck, Bruce Forsyth and Dickie Henderson. From the world of politics came Edward Heath, future Conservative Prime Minister, Clement Atlee, Labour Prime Minister from 1945 to 1951, George Woodcock, General Secretary of the TUC, and Jennie Lee, wife of the great socialist orator and Minister for Health in the 1940s Aneurin Bevan. Also from the world of politics came Jeremy Thorpe, leader of the Liberal Party, and Harold Wilson when he was Labour Prime Minister. From the world of sport came the tennis players Mike Sangster, Bobby Wilson, Mark Cox, Ann Jones, and Sue Barker accompanied by Cliff Richard during their brief romance, with the commentators Fred Perry (over 40 years after he had come as a player), Dan Maskell and Lance Tingay of the *Daily Telegraph*, and perhaps most famous of all Martina Navratilova. Also from the world of sport came the great England bowler Alec Bedser. He travelled to the hotel with the Gloucestershire batsman Crapp.

When Crapp arrived at reception the girl looked up and said,

Bed, sir?
No, Crapp.
Second on the left, sir.

said the receptionist and returned to her ledger.

Omar Sharif.   *Harold Wilson*

Jeremy Thorpe.   *Martina Navratilova*

Margaret   *Snowdon*

Lord Goodman came as did another Lord with a showy blonde who complained noisily and deliberately. He was followed by a private investigator and of course was remembered. This was in the days when adultery was one of the few ways of securing a divorce.

A couple who ultimately found divorce relatively easy, a commentary in itself on how times were changing, were Princess Margaret and Lord Snowdon. In happier days they also came to the Grand.

Mrs Davenport of Davenports Brewery came with her son, who started his day with a goblet of gin and who carried a gun. Colonel Whitbread, who did so much to make Schweppes a great company, came to the hotel to recover from an attack of pneumonia. He sat in the lounge one afternoon after lunch, saying, "I think I'll have a cigarette" and died.

Maxwell Joseph, the man who built up the huge hotel group

Grand Metropolitan, came, and from the world of literature so did Russell Braddon. Also from the world of literature came Lady Antonia Fraser with her second husband Harold Pinter. She wrote of the Grand,

> My husband — Harold Pinter — and I stayed there together on three occasions in the winter in order to write and he stayed there once on his own. He wrote part of the screenplay for 'The French Lieutenant's Woman' and 'Betrayal'; I wrote part of King Charles II.
> On one occasion I remember we occupied the suite in which Debussy wrote 'La Mer'.
> We both appreciated the quietness of the rooms with their high ceilings and thick walls; and of course the wintry view of the sea.

The businessmen came: Lord Sieff from Marks and Spencer and Sir Jack Cohen from Tesco. Sir Jack and Lady Cohen would give a big champagne party on Christmas Day on the first floor gallery and it was a matter of some importance to many guests that they were invited. Mrs Grade, mother of the famous theatrical Grades came and Bill Stapley remembers that she would take fruit up to her room from the dining room to save the service charge. Perhaps that is why her sons are millionaires!

Angela Fox in her book *Slightly Foxed* tells a wonderful story of Mrs Grade at the Grand,

> All the boys were inordinantly proud of their mother. Once, when Leslie and Audrey were spending the weekend with us, Leslie wanted to drive over to Eastbourne to visit his mother where she was on holiday. He didn't want to go without letting her know, so he telephoned the hotel and asked to speak to Mrs Grade.
> "Mrs Grade? Mrs Grade? We have nobody of that name here."
> "Don't be silly. She's my mother and I booked the suite for her, she's my guest."
> This argument persisted for some time, the telephonist at

the Grand Hotel denying the presence of any Mrs Grade and Leslie becoming positively irate until, finally, he demanded to speak to the manager. The manager asked him to hold on while he investigated. He returned in due course to say, "Well, sir, we do have a Mrs Grade-Delfont staying in the hotel. Would that be the lady to whom you are referring?"

"I'm not *referring*," bellowed Leslie. "She's my mother!" By this time Robin and I had got the giggles but Leslie had lost all humour and slammed down the receiver, only to pick it up at once and dial the same number again. This time he asked to be put through to Mrs Grade-Delfont. Mother answered the telephone to hear "Wotchya playing at, Mother? Wotchya doin' to me? I been looking for you. I couldn't find you. What is this Mrs Grade-Delfont?"

Mother was quite unmoved. "Well, Leslie, I wanted them to know that *all* my sons are doing well."

Lord Thompson came in 1964 perhaps for a rest from his Herculean labours with the Scottish newspaper *The Scotsman*, which he had bought after returning to his native land from a lifetime in Canada, and with his independent television channel in Scotland which had prompted his famous remark that independent television was "a licence to print money". Lord Thompson was to go on to even greater things — huge investment and success in North Sea oil, the founding of Thompson Holidays and the purchase of *The Times* and *The Sunday Times*. Perhaps he was getting some fresh sea air and some cosseting at the Grand Hotel before he launched himself on all that.

Also from the business world in 1955 came Francis Ogilvy, father of the David Ogilvy who was to go on to build up the world-famous advertising agency Ogilvy Mather. Madison Avenue was taken by storm by this able and forthright Scot. Mr Ogilvy wrote to Dick Beattie saying that someone had stolen his coat, though not his hat,

> presumably because I take a seven and three quarter in hats which is not much good to most people.

We are reminded of the gentleman who came to dinner at the

Grand and when he was leaving was handed his hat by the porter.

> How do you know that is my hat?
> I don't, sir, but it's the one you were wearing when you came in.

And from the business world came Mr Smith of Smith's Crisps and each year would give Joe Morris, the head floor waiter, a big metal tin of Smith's Crisps. He was joined by Mr Gomme of Gomme Holdings and many of the Mosses of Moss Bros. Monty Moss, chairman of Moss Bros, remembers one Christmas Eve when his jovial father was wearing a funny hat much to the disapproval of his stern mother. She leant across the table and angrily knocked his silly green hat off. Unfortunately Mr Moss senior had an exactly similar one, this time red, underneath. This only served to make Mrs Moss even angrier and the rest of the Moss family more hysterical.

In the mid 1960s for four successive years Charlie Chaplin's

The Chaplin children on Michael Myers' horse.

Dear George Henri

thank you for the

lovely rides. see you

soon These carrots

are for you

love Jane Chaplin

love annette Chaplin

*The letter which the Chaplin
children wrote to the horse.*

children came with their two nannies. Alice Riding, the house-keeper, remembers them as being beautifully mannered. Charlie with his wife Oonagh came just once.

And of course there was the occasional eccentric. Dr Anthony Churcher, the hotel doctor, remembers two of them.

The first was a millionaire from Surrey who would come to the hotel with his valet and personal physician. He would travel down in his night shirt and if he wanted to attend to nature would order his chauffer to stop the Rolls. The commode would then be put against the back door and he would alight and be shielded from public view by a rug.

Totally autocratic, this millionaire liked to order everyone around without question. A wife of two weeks who suggested they might have a holiday was told to have one and not come back.

The second of Dr Churcher's eccentric patients was a parson who was fond of hunting and who used to arrive at the hotel in an Aston Martin. He weighed 20 stone and had a hiatus hernia which gave him pains in his chest after a good meal. One night the doctor was invited to dinner which proved to be champagne and lobster although the parson's wife ordered lobster and poached egg but without the lobster.

This parson loved the Grand and told Dr Churcher he found the hotel telephone operators the most efficient he had known for contacting his book-makers. He loved the Grand so much that he turned his rectory dining room into a replica of the Grand Hotel dining room. When Dr Churcher asked him how he managed to spend so many weekends at the Grand and away from his parishioners the parson told him that he arranged for a mini bus to collect them and take them to a neighbouring church.

The doctor obviously had a certain skill in finding potentially amusing ecclesiastical incidents. He wrote to Alice Riding in 1984,

> Dear Mrs Riding,
> Please could the Rev. Salmon of 137 have bed board.
> Acute back precipitated by going to see the Archbishop last Thursday.
>
> Yours sincerely
> Anthony Churcher

And we all thought the Church had given up corporal punishment!

FILM AND TELEVISION AT THE GRAND

The Grand also welcomed the TV crews and the film world. The hotel with its beautiful façade and spacious, elegant rooms provided the perfect setting for Dennis Potter's 'Cream in My Coffee' (Dennis Potter also wrote 'The Singing Detective', which appeared so successfully on BBC television in 1986) which starred those three famous actors, Peggy Ashcroft (now Dame Peggy Ashcroft), Lionel Jefferies and Martin Shaw. Also shot at the hotel in 1974 was the film *Moments* with Keith Michell and Angharad Rees. According to Alice Riding, the film was not much good but the stars were very nice and she remembers that a helicopter the crew wanted to use to film into a room would not work so they used a crane instead.

THE SUNSHINE RECORDER

Instrumental in bringing guests not only to the Grand but also to Eastbourne has been the sunshine recorder situated on the roof of the central tower block. The recorder dates back to 1880, not long after the hotel was built, and every day an employee of the local corporation has taken the lift to the third floor and then a private staircase to the roof and noted the results of the previous day from the recorder. The results have then been displayed in the showcase at the Central Bandstand. Jack Breach remarked in 1967,

> That glass ball on the roof of the Grand is worth its weight in gold to this town. For the past 6 years Eastbourne has been the sunniest mainland resort.

QUALITY STILL COUNTS

The Grand Hotel had changed, had been forced to change. Dick Beattie had realised the necessity as had his successors Norman Brooke and John Welsh and the new owners De Vere Hotels. De Vere had spent heavily on refurbishment and on installing many more rooms with private bathrooms. The five star status of the hotel had been restored and at the end of the 1970s the Grand could face the future with confidence. Or could it?

CHAPTER NINE

ROLLER-COASTER THROUGH THE SEVENTIES AND EIGHTIES

THE CUSTOMER APOLOGISED TO HIM!

The Grand could indeed face the future with confidence in 1970. The world economy was apparently in good shape, and the British economy, after a mixed performance in the late 1960s, seemed poised to join it. A new Conservative government under Edward Heath had been elected in June 1970, promising lower taxes and less interference in business generally. However, under the surface, all was not well, and the 1970s proved to be a bad decade for Britain. The rate of inflation had started to accelerate in the 1960s as successive governments, Conservative and Labour, pursued a policy of maintaining full employment at all costs. This was the avowed, and in many ways worthy, aim of all politicians after the war. No one wanted a return to the high unemployment levels of the 1930s, and each government implemented Keynesian policies of keeping demand high, using (if necessary, and especially at election times) public money to prime the economic pump. The result, especially in Britain with some archaic industrial management and workforce practices, was the creation of greater demand than supply – the classic cause of inflation. The general index of retail prices, which had risen only 0.5% in 1959 and 1.1% in 1960, was accelerating at 4.7% in 1968 and 5.4% in 1969. This was fine for business, and luxury hotels such as the Grand, as long as inflation did not accelerate.

However, the late 1960s was just a foretaste of what was to come in the 1970s. The Conservatives pumped money into the economy as never before in 1971 and 1972, following the news that unemployment had broken through the one million barrier, considered an appalling number at the time. Unfortunately, Britain's expansion coincided with a world boom. In 1971 the United States turned from being an exporter of oil into a net importer; and in October 1973, when yet another Arab-Israeli conflict, the Yom Kippur War, broke out, the Arab oil producers chose the moment to quadruple the price of oil and to cut back production. The effect on world trade was little short of disastrous.

The world, and especially the UK, suffered a deep recession accompanied by high rates of inflation in the mid-1970s. At one point in 1975, the UK's annual inflation rate was running at a frightening 25%. Overall prices tripled between 1970 and 1979, while taxes remained high. This banished for ever, except in a few isolated cases, the upper class that could afford a string of servants and months in an English hotel by the sea. If the Grand had ever been reliant on that market, it was never going to be so in the future.

The future for the Grand lay in conferences, while private clients coming at Easter, Whitsun, the summer and Christmas were seen almost as a bonus. Norman Brooke, who took over as manager from Dick Beattie in 1965, and John Welsh, who succeeded Brooke in October 1973, both realised the importance of the conference business to the Grand's success. Brooke began his hotel career at the Mayfair Hotel in London, before becoming assistant manager at the Metropole in

Brighton, the Grosvenor at Victoria in London and the Mayfair. He had also served as deputy to the famous hotelier Michael Chapman, at the Imperial Torquay. During his managership at the Grand, the hotel regained its five-star status, which had been lost in the 1960s primarily because of its low number of en-suite rooms.

John Welsh, like Brooke a member of the Réunion des Gastronomes, came to the Grand after running the Branksome Towers near Bournemouth. His experience included managing hotels in Bermuda and Jamaica, as well as the Royal Albion and Adelphi in Brighton. Described as more of a 'front man' than the slightly nervous and perhaps somewhat autocratic Brooke, Welsh's forte was making the guests feel at home. Roy Atfield, who served the Grand from 1955 until 1999, mainly as the room service manager, told the author in June 2000:

> John Welsh was the only manager I knew that could handle a complaining customer so that in the end the customer would be apologising to him!

Unfortunately for Welsh, his managership coincided with the recession of the mid-1970s and another one in the early 1980s. In 1983 he was succeeded by Peter Hawley, who was promoted from a successful eight-year stint as manager of the Queen's Hotel in Eastbourne, also owned by De Vere. Hawley, at 35, was the youngest ever manager at the Grand. His appointment coincided with De Vere's decision to invest £750,000 in a refurbishment programme shortly after he arrived. Such investment was long overdue.

Orchard Interiors, well-known for their work on department stores including Harrods, used pastel shades and rich velours to bring the hotel from the 1960s to the 1980s. Appreciating how vital conference business was to the hotel, De Vere also spent £250,000 on the Devonshire Suite. Designed at the end of the nineteenth century as a Victorian ballroom, it was already a perfect auditorium and De Vere now made it an ideal conference room by adding air-conditioning, a broadcasting quality sound system and sophisticated theatre lighting.

The designers were Theatre Projects Limited, known for their lighting of many West End productions, including *Starlight Express*. Finally, the original stage was replaced by a portable stage.

Hawley was rewarded by strong growth in conference bookings. Such leading companies as Ford, IBM, 3M, British Airways and Calor Gas came year after year, as did the accountants Cooper and Lybrand, Price Waterhouse and Touche Ross, and many of the country's largest building societies. Roy Atfield remembered having to serve 15 dinner parties, all with separate bars in suites, for the Cooper and Lybrand conference year after year.

Perhaps the greatest excitement came with the record companies, CBS, Polygram and Virgin, who all held "bashes" in September 1988. This brought such well-known names as Wham, Spandau Ballet, Alison Moyet, Jennifer Rush, Paul Young, George Harrison and Freddie Mercury (who would drink only Cristal champagne – as the hotel had only two bottles in stock, it was necessary to rush in some more).

Not all celebrities drink champagne. When Hawley showed Wham singers George Michael and Andrew Ridgeley, who had arrived by helicopter, to their suites, he said: "You will find a bottle of champagne in your room." Michael replied, "We don't want champagne. We want some coke." Hawley duly sent up four bottles of Coca-Cola on ice!

However, as well as aiming at conferences and famous customers, Hawley was also keen to bring in people who lived in Eastbourne, and said:

> We are also deeply interested in attracting local residents to wine and dine with us at the Grand. Our prices are reasonable – dinner from £12.50, lunch from £7.50 and afternoon tea served in the Great Hall £3.50, all with a warm, receptive welcome.

GREENALL WHITLEY BUYS DE VERE ——————

Hawley was hardly installed in the Grand when the De Vere Group was bought by the brewery group, Greenall Whitley. Greenall Whitley had been founded over 200 years earlier by Thomas Greenhalgh. He changed his name to Greenall and his grand-daughter, Isabella, married John Whitley. Hence Greenall Whitley. The company had gradually prospered in the North West of England, and by the 1970s was ready to expand into hotels and other leisure activities.

The Rt. Hon. Margaret Thatcher, considered by many Britain's most influential twentieth-century Prime Minister, almost lost her life at The Grand Hotel, Brighton. The Grand Hotel in Eastbourne made sure there would be no bombs in their hotel. (Photograph courtesy of Popperfoto.)

One of the first investments in the Grand made by the new owners was a leisure centre in the basement of the hotel. It included a swimming pool, spa bath, sauna, solarium and gymnasium, and was opened in September 1985 by Ian Gow, Eastbourne's Conservative MP and Minister of State at the Treasury (later to be murdered by the IRA). The first to dive into the pool was Olympic silver medallist, Sharron Davies.

However, before this, Peter Hawley's diplomatic and managerial skills had been tested by a proposed visit from Prime Minister Margaret Thatcher, in November 1984. She was due to come, plus 50 other Members of Parliament, to the CBI conference at Eastbourne to answer questions from businessmen, and she and most of the MPs were due to stay at the Grand.

Peter Hawley with Yehudi Menuhin, who helped launch music weekends at The Grand.

In October 1984 the Grand Hotel in Brighton (also part of the Greenall Whitley Group), where the Prime Minister and many of the Cabinet had been staying during the Conservative Party conference, had been blown up with the loss of four lives. It was the closest the country had ever come to losing the entire Cabinet.

In the light of this event, the security precautions for the visit to Eastbourne were intense. Every member of the hotel staff was issued with an identity tag with a photograph, and the police planned to go through the hotel with sniffer dogs early in the morning on the day of the Prime Minister's visit.

On Sunday morning, 4 November 1984, one of the sniffer dogs discovered a 5lb tin of Quality Street chocolates behind the lavatory in the bathroom of room 101. Peter Hawley and a senior police officer were called. Both agreed that it was suspicious, and the East Wing of the hotel was quietly cleared between 8.30 and 9.00 am. Electronic equipment was brought in, and shortly afterwards it was reported to Peter in the Main Hall that the test showed positive. There was now no alternative but to clear the hotel, and quickly. The fire bells were sounded, and 250 guests were shepherded out of the hotel, some of them still in their pyjamas. Within minutes only Peter Hawley, a telephonist and the police were left.

The guests went to the Cavendish and the Queen's Hotel and to a local college, where they had to break in because no one could find a key. Meanwhile, an area around the hotel was cordoned off and everyone waited for the bomb disposal squad from Ashford. Peter Hawley remembers vividly the police telling him he would soon be faced with the dilemma of asking the bomb disposal unit either to dismantle the bomb or to blow it up, and probably half of the East Wing with it. While he was pondering, the police came and told him that an X-ray of the tin showed that it was a hoax – the tin was full of strips of expanded polystyrene.

The relief was enormous. Nevertheless, the whole hotel was

searched and an "X" was marked on each room door as it was cleared. By three o'clock in the afternoon the all-clear was given, and the management were then faced with the task of organising the departure of all their Saturday night guests, the cleaning of the rooms, and the arrival of the conference delegates.

A reception area was set up at the Congress Theatre, and the arrivals were temporarily diverted there. Miraculously, by six o'clock in the evening the whole transfer was achieved and the incoming delegates expressed their amazement that their rooms were ready so quickly. Mrs Alice Riding was heard to say: "I hope Mr Hawley doesn't think I'm going to clean the hotel every day in three hours."

After all this excitement, the Prime Minister did not in fact come to the conference. She had been to the funeral of the Indian Prime Minster, Mrs Gandhi, in India (also the victim of violence), and it was felt she could not get back in time.

Who planted the bomb? Some cynics suggested it might have been someone from the press, to test whether the police would find it. Other cynics suggested it might have been the police themselves, to show the public (after the undiscovered bomb at Brighton) that they were effective at finding planted bombs. But no one knows for sure, and no one was ever arrested.

MUSIC AND THE GRAND HOTEL

We have already seen how important music had been to the Grand, and Hawley was determined that the hotel's association with music should be revived. He organised special weekends devoted to music lovers. On a weekend in April 1984, the Hungarian pianist Peter Frankl came to the Grand to give a recital. During the same weekend, the Royal Philharmonic Orchestra played at the Congress Theatre, conducted by Yehudi Menuhin. On the Sunday, a "Palm Court" orchestra played in the Hall from 11.00 to 12.30, and as in the golden era of the

Grand Hotel Orchestra, the men in the audience were requested to wear black ties.

The weekend was a great success, and was followed by similar weekends which aimed to provide serious but popular music with a broad appeal, in an atmosphere of luxury and comfort second to none on the South Coast.

THE STORMS OF 1987

The next big excitement for Hawley and his team were the storms of October 1987. It was a double whammy, as near-hurricanes swept first through the south of England and second through the world's financial markets three days later. On Thursday 15 October, the BBC weather forecast predicted nothing more than a windy night. What happened in reality was something no one in the south of England had ever experienced before. Seve Ballesteros, the Open and Masters champion, who was playing at Wentworth, walked from the house where he was staying to the club house on the Friday morning, climbed his way over hundreds of uprooted trees and thought that possibly the world had ended. The storms that swept across the southern half of the country caused hundreds of millions of pounds' worth of damage, and Eastbourne was as badly hit as anywhere.

At the Grand, the hotel was hosting 300 members of the National Association of Fruit and Potato Traders at their annual conference. Even by Saturday evening, when a big banquet was planned, the hotel still had no electricity. However, as always, the staff rallied round, and a restricted menu was served by gaslight. Lindsay Cooper, who has served the hotel on the front office and sales side for 22 years, remembers that she drove Jonathan Webley, now manager of the Grand but then deputy manager, to pick up a new car, his first-ever brand new car. When they arrived, the car had been severely damaged by the

Eastbourne's famous tree-lined avenues suffered severely in the storms of October 1987.

storms. Webley was understandably upset.

Following damage to the fabric of the hotel (mostly to the roof), the management's next problem was leaks caused by the heavy rainfall which followed in the days after the storm. The author remembers that he visited the hotel in the following week, and was asked by Peter Hawley to go and knock on people's bedroom doors on the top floor at 11.30 pm to see if their ceilings were leaking. It was a memorable but perhaps not to be repeated experience.

The author also remembers Peter Hawley expressing concern that all of his clients had been wiped out by the hurricane that had swept through the world's financial markets. Investors had been feeling very pleased with themselves in the summer of 1987. The Thatcher (and in the USA, the Reagan) bull markets had been roaring away since the early 1980s, and in the UK Margaret Thatcher had just been re-elected. Money, serious money, was there for the taking, and after the usual summer hiccup, the indices were going up again when BANG! It all stopped. First New York, then London, then New York again, then Hong Kong, Tokyo and Sydney, then London, Paris and Frankfurt all turned into screaming pits of hysteria as the markets lost a year's gains in 24 hours.

It was only 12 years, or 3,000 trading days, since the FT30 Index had stood at 147. Now it lost 183.7 in a single day. The Dow Jones fell by over 500 points, and it was only five years since that index had been around 600. There was real concern, even panic in some quarters, but within days the market steadied and, as so often happens, taking the long-term, even the medium-term view, it was a great buying opportunity. And Hawley's customers did not desert him. Indeed, the Grand enjoyed bumper years in 1988 and 1989, before the going became tougher in the early 1990s as another recession hit the UK. Perhaps the crash of 1987 had been signalling something after all.

THE MIRABELLE RESTAURANT ──────────────────

In 1989, the De Vere group allocated Hawley £400,000 to establish another restaurant in the Grand, prompted by a warning from the AA that the hotel might lose its five-star status if it could not offer guests the choice of two restaurants. It had also become clear that the very success of the conference business was proving detrimental to private client bookings, as the conferences tended to take over the hotel and other guests were not sure where they would be eating from one meal to the next.

At the east end of the hotel, in the former rooms 6, 7, 8 and 9, one of which had been the board room of the old Grand Hotel company, the Mirabelle Restaurant was created, and soon established itself as one of the finest restaurants in the south of England.

Shortly after the opening of the Mirabelle, the dreaded recession arrived as the early 1990s mirrored the early 1980s. The glorious boom years of the 1980s ended in bust. The stock market crash of 1987 had not slowed down the British economy, and by the middle of 1988 it was clear that it was overheating badly. Chancellor of the Exchequer Nigel (now Lord) Lawson raised interest rates sharply until they reached 15%, meaning that many people and businesses were paying 18-20% on their overdrafts, mortgages and loans. There could only be one consequence of this. Many people and businesses were bankrupted, and everyone had to forgo their easy spending habits of a year or two earlier. When people complained about the high interest rate policy, Lawson's replacement as Chancellor, John Major, said: "If it isn't hurting, it isn't working."

It was certainly hurting many people. After three or four very difficult years Peter Hawley decided to move on, and in 1994 he bought the Chatsworth Hotel, situated a few minutes' walk along King Edward's Parade. When asked to recall some of the more eccentric moments of his time as manager, Hawley remembered the cat-loving boss whose retirement dinner at the Grand was a roaring success. His colleagues brought a special guest, a tiger from Chipperfield's Circus. Then there was the leading British company which decided that its delegates need not have "posh nosh" every night, and gave them fish and chips wrapped up in the *Financial Times*. On another occasion, hard-up members of the Russian Ballet had their accommodation paid for them, but could not afford any food. Staff discovered them cooking food over tiny stoves in their rooms. Finally, the electrical wholesalers decided on a medieval theme for their annual dinner, with a baby elephant as the highlight.

Peter Hawley was succeeded by Jonathan Webley, his former deputy manager, who had subsequently enjoyed a successful spell as manager of another De Vere hotel in Coventry.

CHAPTER TEN

"A HUGE CREAMY PALACE"

A BAPTISM OF FIRE

Jonathan Webley took over in June 1994. At the time, at the age of 34, he was the youngest manager of a five-star hotel in the UK. Exactly a year later, his mettle was tested to the full. On Monday 26 June 1995, an assistant housekeeper called him to a fifth-floor room where workmen had been repainting, using blow torches to strip off the old paint. Her suspicions had been aroused by evidence that a hose had been used to douse a fire. Although there was a smell of smoke, the fire alarm had not gone off and there were no flames. However, Webley was not prepared to take any chances, and using his mobile telephone (which he had just acquired), he summoned the fire brigade and gave orders for the hotel to be evacuated. (Later, as the blaze was tackled by the fire brigade, the water put the telecommunications systems out of action, and his mobile phone became the only means of communication with the outside world.)

It was just as well that he did raise the alarm, because within minutes flames broke out on the roof and a major disaster loomed. However, the fire brigades of East Sussex acted promptly, and within minutes 15 appliances from Eastbourne,

Lewes, Uckfield, Seaford, Rosedean, Bexhill and Newhaven were on their way. The fire spread quickly, partly because of the hidden roof voids in the Victorian structure. East Sussex assistant county fire officer, Terry Johns, said later:

> It was a very severe fire and travelled very quickly. The tar and pitch in the roof contributed to the blaze and there is a hole about 20 metres square in the roof.

Fortunately, the danger to the whole hotel was averted, and Webley remembers that the firemen were very conscious of preservation while they were bringing the fire under control. Nevertheless, in the short term, business would be lost. The Association of District Councils was due to start its conference in the hotel on Wednesday 28 June. As always, the staff were magnificent, and Webley said later:

The fire of June 1995 could have been catastrophic, but for the quick reactions of the management, staff and the fire brigade.

Quite frankly, what happened here on Tuesday was incredible. All the staff came in in the morning ready for the clean up and we assigned them different jobs. All the furniture was taken out to the gardens to give it a good airing, and it was a massive spring clean involving around 150 staff. By 4 pm the hotel was no longer a disaster area and we were back operating as a hotel.

The Grand worked together with the organisers of the Association of District Councils conference to find alternative accommodation for those delegates whose rooms were affected. The ADC conference's annual dinner was moved to the Cavendish Hotel, but delegates were back at the Grand for the start of the conference on the Wednesday morning. The Mayor of Eastbourne wrote to Webley on the Thursday:

Dear Jonathan,
   I was able to express to you yesterday the sincerest thanks of the Chairman of the Association of District Councils for all the work which was undertaken by staff at the Grand Hotel on the occasion of the disastrous fire this week.
   I would like formally to couple my thanks with those of the Chairman of Conference and to express the appreciation of the whole town for the manner in which the problems of guests were resolved.
   Would you be so kind, please, as to ensure that our best thanks are extended to all your staff with regard to this incident.

There were, of course, short-term consequences. For example, the Football Association conference, due to come to the Grand the following weekend, was transferred to the Royal Bath in Bournemouth, a sister De Vere hotel, and with 40 rooms out of action from June until November, Webley mourned his lost business. In August he said:

It is frustrating that I have not got all my rooms because the demand is so great we are turning people away.

William Hague, leader of the Conservative Party, is greeted on the steps of the Grand by Jonathan Webley.

Graeme Bateman (right), managing director of Elite Hotels, and Jonathan Webley, general manager of the Grand Hotel, shortly after Elite acquired the Grand.

Tylney Hall (top) and Ashdown Park, Elite Hotels' other properties.

However, all was not doom and gloom. The fire triggered a complete bedroom refurbishment as Webley, taking advantage of the recovering economy, settled down to lure back those customers lost in the recession of the early 1990s. And he was successful. As well as a number of the leading firms in the country, the Grand attracted guests for the Liberal Democrat conference in September 1997 and the Labour conference on Europe in November 1997, as well as new Tory leader William Hague and his shadow cabinet and key national party members for a strategy meeting in October of that year. (The Tories' long 18 years of power had come to an end in May 1997 when Labour, led by the youthful Tony Blair, swept in with a large majority.)

This meeting of the Tory hierarchy brought a great deal of publicity, partly because of the varying styles of dress that the MPs wore. Some were in three-piece suits, others in woolly jumpers. However, the meeting was obviously deemed a success and the Grand was also rewarded for its excellence, because the strategy team returned the following year. "Grunge" gear was out and smart country gear was in, with plenty of moss-coloured sports jackets, beige cords and slacks with brogues. William Hague, just returned from a weekend in Rome with his new wife, Ffion, arrived in a green sports jacket, beige trousers, brogues, blue shirt and yellow patterned tie. Whatever their manner of attire, the Tories were still clearly shattered by their defeat in May 1997, and most pundits reckoned it would be many years before they were ready to challenge for power again.

ELITE HOTELS

Between the two Tory strategy sessions, a momentous event happened at the Grand. On 12 February 1998, Jonathan Webley was summoned to a meeting by the De Vere directors and told that the group was in discussion with Elite Hotels, which would probably lead to the Elite group buying the Grand. And indeed, on 31 March 1998, that was what happened.

Elite Hotels (Rotherwick) Ltd. had been formed in 1992, and at that time owned the Tylney Hall Hotel in Rotherwick, near Hook in Hampshire, a beautiful country house hotel. In 1993 the group bought the equally exquisite Ashdown Park near Forest Row in Sussex.

The Grand Hotel was its next acquisition. Elite would have been pleased by the reaction in Eastbourne. David Elkin, Chairman of the Eastbourne Hotels Association, said: "It's very good for the town. It's such a compliment to Eastbourne."

Graeme Bateman, managing director of Elite, said that the Grand matched the profile of its existing hotels. He also talked immediately of extensive renovations and remodelling of the hotel to cater for twenty-first century needs. Clagues, architects

Graeme Bateman, managing director of Elite Hotels,
the delighted new owners of the Grand.

from Canterbury, were instrumental in bringing the vision alive, whilst preserving the heritage.

Bateman said:

> We will pay attention to details. We will reduce the number of bedrooms, improve the standard of furnishings and leisure facilities and give the restaurant a higher profile. Obviously it is a very fine building in its own right but we want to make it even more deluxe.

And refurbish the Grand Elite certainly did. Bateman described the whole exercise as very absorbing – "As a company we do not use interior designers, preferring the personal approach" – and very exciting: "We discovered wonderful ceilings when we stripped away false ones built in the 1960s, and in the Devonshire Suite when we stripped away plaster we found the original colours were the same as the ones we had chosen."

Bateman knew that refurbishment, which was very extensive and would last from July 1998 until March 2000, would be wearing on staff morale, and the first thing that was done was to buy a small hotel in nearby Jevington Gardens and convert it into modern staff accommodation to replace the existing cramped and outdated staff quarters in the basement of the Grand. The building company used to carry out the refurbishment was Cardy Construction, based in Canterbury. Cardy had worked on both Tylney Hall and Ashdown Park, and Bateman knew they could be trusted to carry out the work to the standard required.

Mike Keatley, who oversaw the work for Cardy and who had done the same at both Tylney Hall and Ashdown Park, told the author in June 2000 that the work carried out at the Grand proved to be "a mammoth task". He was almost overawed by the sheer size of everything – the doors, the windows, the staircases. The old swimming pool in the Leisure Club, now renamed the Health Club, had to be dug out by hand and eight tonnes of structural steel manhandled in to support the new and larger swimming pool. In the Devonshire Suite, 25 tonnes of structural steel was used. We have seen earlier that the Grand was completely re-wired in 1933. This was the first time that a complete re-wiring had taken place since then. Keatley remembered that throughout the 18 months both the Grand's maintenance and management teams were extremely helpful, though he could not help noticing that some of them were clearly worried and wondering what these people were doing to their hotel. The hotel remained open throughout the refurbishment, and Keatley said:

> Working on occupied premises requires a lot of planning and we are working very closely with the hotel management. This often means liaising on an hourly, rather than a daily basis.

When the project was completed, Cardy quoted a few statistics showing just what had been involved. The team of 35 builders and 100 contractors clocked up 197,600 man-hours, 20,000 glazed tiles were fitted in the new hotel bathrooms, 250 steel lintels, weighing 30 tonnes, were used to support ceilings and door frames, and 43,734 metres of timber and 69,333 metres of cable were also used. And it needed 704 skips to remove rubble and building rubbish.

One of the first exercises for Cardy was the refurbishment of the bedrooms, which included the reduction of the number of rooms from 164 to 152, as the small single rooms were eradicated. Anyone staying on their own would automatically be allocated a double room. On 24 May 1999, an army of 50 staff and contractors changed all the numbers on the bedroom doors. It meant that guests staying in the Grand at the time checked in under one number and checked out under another. Jonathan Webley could see the slightly farcical side to this exercise, but said at the time:

> There may be a few people who might forget which room they are staying in, but we have been planning this for months and will do everything to ensure it goes as smoothly as possible.

The Presidential Suite master bedroom.

The award-winning Mirabelle Restaurant, which has added a new dimension to the hotel.

The Chatsworth Lounge, now restored to its former glory with the original ceiling and magnificent pillars exposed again.

The Garden Restaurant with its mirrored sliding doors, based on an idea from Luton Hoo.

The swimming pool in the Health Club, which also includes a gym, eight beauty treatment rooms, a hairdressing salon, steam rooms and saunas.

The Devonshire Suite, on three floors, offers comprehensive, self-contained conference and dining facilities.

By June 1999, much of the work in the hotel had been completed. Two of the major sites were the main conference suite and the health club. The Devonshire Suite, the hotel's main conference area, now comprised the conference room (renamed the Compton Room) and additional facilities on the mezzanine and lower ground floor, an area previously used for staff accommodation. The Jevington Lounge on the mezzanine had its own bar, reception area and four meeting rooms, while the Silverdale Room on the lower ground floor provided banqueting facilities for up to 200 people.

The Grand Hotel Health Club included an enlarged pool and gym area, eight beauty treatment rooms, a hairdressing salon, steam rooms and saunas for both men and women. For the first time, guests could go directly to the outdoor pool from the health club.

To celebrate the year's successful construction work, on 20 June 1999 Elite Hotels held a champagne reception for 300 people, including Eastbourne Mayor Beryl Healy and local MP Nigel Waterson. Graeme Bateman said to the assembled guests:

> With the major part of the refurbishment programme nearing completion, we have realised our ambition to complete the main part of our programme within 12 months of its commencement. As you will see for yourselves this afternoon, this has been no easy task. Indeed, it is wrong to simplify this as any normal refurbishment. Elite Hotels inherited a very tired old lady. Behind the scenes we have removed the numerous single rooms that were an insult to the five-star grading. The plumbing, electrics, and fire protection systems have been replaced, ensuring that the hotel is well placed to meet the demands and expectations of tomorrow's guests.
>
> I would like to pay particular thanks to Jonathan for his support during the last year. He and his family have had to endure much. Living here inside the building, they have suffered many sleepless nights as we have surged towards each deadline. I am sure you will agree, Jonathan, it has been fun as well as hard work – bet you had no idea what was in store when we first met in January last year!

Finally, I would like to apologise to those of you who have been dragged away from your Father's Day celebrations, London to Brighton Bike Ride and not least, final of the Cricket World Cup.

The guests might not have been too happy if England had been in the final. Sadly, they had not even reached the knock-out stage. In the event, the final was a one-sided affair, with Australia beating Pakistan easily.

And the work went on. The next completed project was the Presidential Suite, which included a York stone balcony, grand sitting room, four-poster bed and huge whirlpool bath. Webley said:

> Many famous people have stayed in this suite, including recently the Queen of Spain and Richard Branson, and we look forward to welcoming many more.

SKILL IS IMPRESSIVE ACROSS ALL DEPARTMENTS

One of the most important areas to benefit from the refurbishment was the restaurants. The Garden Restaurant was completely redecorated. Out went the murals that had been painted in the panels in the late 1980s, out went the dividers, and a wall with sliding mirrored doors – based on an idea from Luton Hoo, at the time being acquired by Elite Hotels – was put in their place. Webley said:

> Even though the name has remained the same, everything else is brand new, from the tables, chairs and décor to Wedgwood china and cut glass … We have reduced the number of tables so there is a more spacious feel.

At the same time, the Mirabelle Restaurant was expanded to include its own bar. And the Grand was winning accolades for its cuisine. Many awards had been won over the previous decade, especially since Keith Mitchell had joined the hotel in 1989. He had become Head Chef of the Mirabelle when it opened in 1990, and the Grand's Executive Chef in 1991. He had been a consistent winner of Salon Culinaire gold medals from 1983 to 1995, and in 1996 he won the prize for the most outstanding entry in the international Malta Grand Prix competition. In that year he also went to Moscow to judge the first international Salon Culinaire to be held in Russia.

Now, in 1999, the restaurant bible, *The Good Food Guide,* awarded the Mirabelle eight out of ten points for its cooking. Only three restaurants received ten points, four received nine points and another seven besides the Mirabelle, eight. The Mirabelle was praised for its "smooth, unhurried and stylish service". The full entry read:

> Menus tend to play down complexity, enabling dishes to deliver more than anticipated. For example, a tumbling pile of seared bass, tuna, red mullet, salmon, scallops and mussels, each species precisely cooked and showing its different characteristics, sitting on a single sheet of black pasta, with a saffron sauce for dramatic contrast, the whole thing crowned with a wanton of lobster.
>
> Many dishes have a multi-dimensional ring to them, requiring skill and precision to make them work. For desserts, one couple, overcome by curiosity, sampled the novelty of a deep-fried blueberry ice-cream perched on a biscuit surrounded by a soup of melon and lemon-grass. Doubts only surfaced about whether they'd made the right choice when they watched a six-inch tall tian of chocolate being delivered to another table.
>
> Skill is impressive across all departments, and is applied equally in appetisers and delicate pastries and petits fours.

And the accolades were not just coming the Mirabelle's way. Elite will have been gratified by the Grand achieving its highest ever percentage award for excellence from the AA in November 1999. The jump from 64 to 70% meant that the Grand had become the top rated five-star resort hotel in the UK. And the rating was improved to 73% in 2000. In June 2000, the Grand won the South East English Tourist Board's award for hotel of the year, with the judges commenting on the country house atmosphere by the sea and commending the Grand's emphasis on staff development and training.

Also in 2000, the Grand announced that it had become a member of the exclusive marketing consortium, Small Luxury Hotels of the World. For 30 years, Small Luxury Hotels had brought together some of the finest hotels throughout the world, and membership guaranteed that guests would enjoy unrivalled levels of luxury, privacy and exclusivity. Graeme Bateman said:

> With the recent inclusion of the Grand we have scored a hat-trick, as all three Elite Hotels are proud to be members of Small Luxury Hotels.

And the news was travelling. *The Independent* said in May 2000:

> There is really only one place to stay. The Grand Hotel sprawling like an imperial wedding cake … is an institution. Kings and queens have stayed, Debussy concluded *La Mer* in one of the bedrooms, Harold Pinter wrote his screenplay for *The French Lieutenant's Woman* here and Winston Churchill and Haile Selassie's names appear regularly in the visitors' book. The late Tommy Cooper ate many Sunday lunches at the Grand and last year I bumped into Eddie Izzard by the lifts – at first mistaking him for a butch middle-aged woman, he may be pleased to learn. … My bed took on a different aura after I was told that Steffi Graf had slept in it during a previous year's Eastbourne tennis week.

Dennis Potter had summed up the Grand beautifully when his television series 'Cream in My Coffee' was filmed in the hotel: "The Grand Hotel is a huge creamy palace."

INDEX

Index

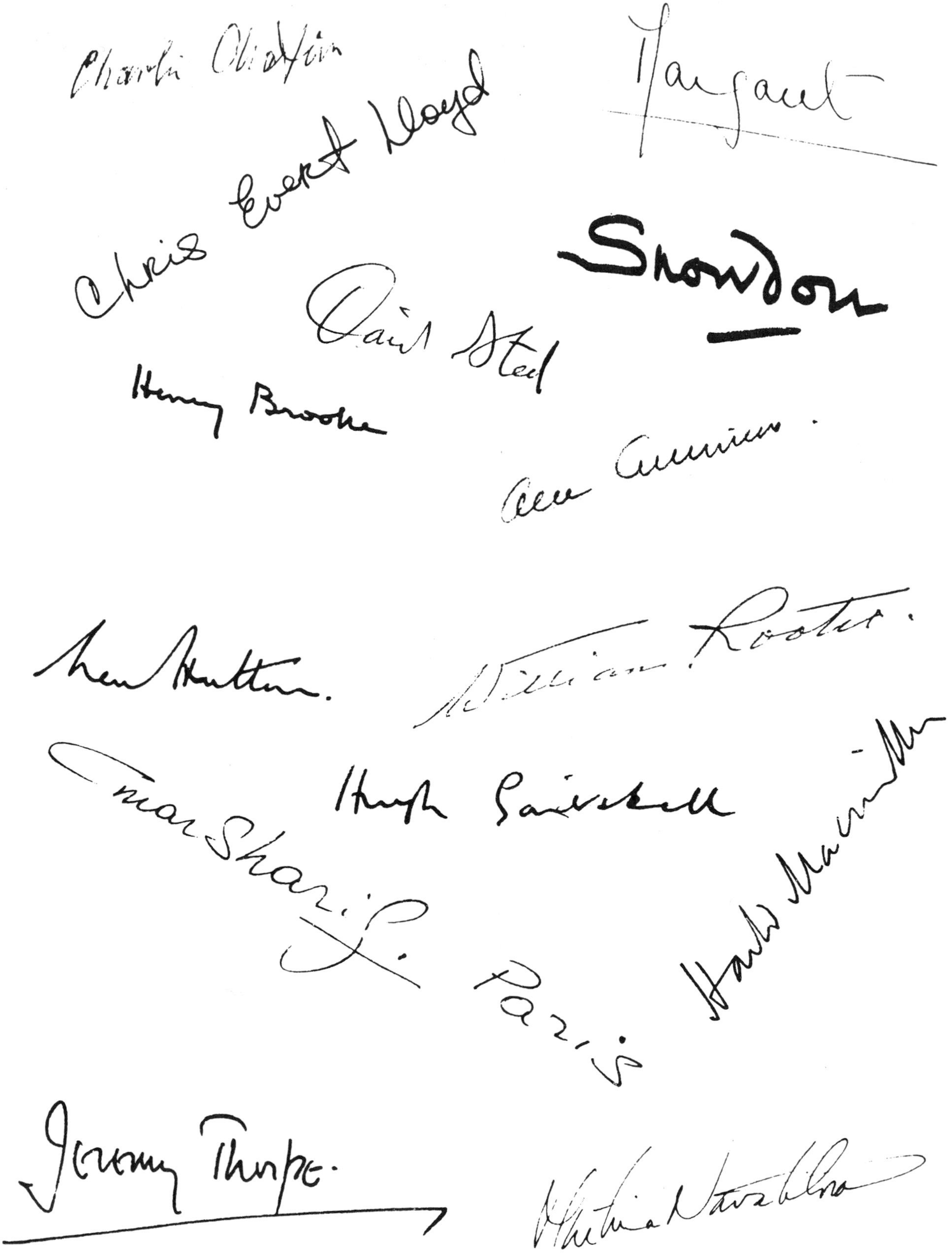

Charlie Chaplin

Chris Evert Lloyd

Margaret

Snowdon

David Steel

Henry Brooke

Alec Cunnium

Len Hutton

William Foster

Hugh Gaitskell

Harold Macmillan

Omar Sharif. Paris

Jeremy Thorpe.

Martina Navratilova